# PRAISE FOR *TOXIC RELATIONSHIP RECOVERY*

"Jaime covers so much ground in this book. I recommend it to anyone who might be questioning their relationship patterns, and to those who are clear about the dysfunction they're experiencing but need concrete tools in order to create sustainable change."
—Ingrid Clayton, PhD, clinical psychologist and author of *Believing Me: Healing from Narcissistic Abuse and Complex Trauma*

"*Toxic Relationship Recovery* offers a practical and accessible approach for individuals seeking to heal past wounds and establish healthier patterns in their relationships. Jaime's exceptional ability to deconstruct the concepts presented in this book—along with the aid of insightful examples—empowers readers to identify and liberate themselves from toxic patterns."
—Dr. Patrice Berry, psychologist and author of *Turning Crisis Into Clarity*

"*Toxic Relationship Recovery* has quickly risen to the top of my recommendation list with clients. Jaime helps the reader find the line between self-advocacy and toxic behavior—a line that is often difficult to discern in high-conflict relationships or after betrayal. This book is a must-read for anyone trying to recalibrate the way they love and connect with others."
—Dr. Kate Balestrieri, psychologist, sex therapist, founder of Modern Intimacy, and host of the *Modern Intimacy* podcast

"Jaime finds a way to make the difficult topic of recovery from a toxic relationship understandable for clinicians and consumers alike. Her ability to normalize these conversations empowers those who are reading to feel like they are no longer alone. Early on, Jaime reminds readers that 'You have value'—this helps set the tone for the healing that can be expected throughout the book."
—Eddie Carrillo, MA, LPC, licensed mental health therapist and cohost of the *Millennial Mental Health Channel* podcast

"Jaime gives you the two essential components required to fully heal from a toxic relationship: a trusted guide and an effective plan. As a therapist and consultant, I will recommend this book to my clients because of Jaime's expertise and her ability to communicate in a warm, engaging manner. She delivers substantial information, and she uses stories and real-world examples to help the information move from your head to your heart."
—Trey Tucker, LPC, MA, therapist, con
Counseling

# PRAISE FOR *TOXIC RELATIONSHIP RECOVERY*

"Healing from the wounds of trauma can be a very difficult journey, but Jaime Mahler's *Toxic Relationship Recovery* is a guiding light toward healing and empowerment. With compassion and wisdom, Jaime shares her profound knowledge and provides a very powerful message for others to navigate the complexities of trauma recovery. *Toxic Relationship Recovery* offers insightful perspectives and practical tools that empower survivors to reclaim their strength and rewrite their narratives. If you or someone you know has been affected by trauma and needs help navigating through tough decisions, *Toxic Relationship Recovery* is an invaluable companion on the journey toward healing and reestablishment."
—Yasmin Regan, trauma survivor

"A companion when life feels impossibly toxic. You don't have to heal alone. Jaime gently guides us from 'That's not normal' to full recovery and rediscovery. I will be reading it twice."
—Qveen Herby, recording artist, @qveenherby

"Both practical and powerful, this book is the definitive guide for understanding and healing from toxic relationships. Jaime puts names to things that most of us experience, yet many of us don't talk about. But now we can."
—Sarah Edmondson, author of *Scarred: The True Story of How I Escaped NXIVM, the Cult That Bound My Life* and host/producer of the *A Little Bit Culty* podcast

"*Toxic Relationship Recovery* should be required reading for all young people, those who have survived toxic relationships and are looking for answers, and anyone interested in psychology. Jaime Mahler masterfully explains this often-overlooked topic in an approachable and nonjudgmental way. We will be recommending this masterpiece for years to come."
—Justin Romano, MD, psychiatrist and cohost of the *Millennial Mental Health Channel* podcast

# TOXIC
## RELATIONSHIP
### Recovery

## JAIME MAHLER, MS, LMHC
### @RecollectedSelf

ADAMS MEDIA
NEW YORK   LONDON   TORONTO   SYDNEY   NEW DELHI

Adams Media
An Imprint of Simon & Schuster, Inc.
100 Technology Center Drive
Stoughton, Massachusetts 02072

First Adams Media trade paperback edition September 2023

For information about special discounts for bulk purchases, please contact Simon & Schuster Special Sales at 1-866-506-1949 or business@simonandschuster.com.

The Simon & Schuster Speakers Bureau can bring authors to your live event. For more information or to book an event, contact the Simon & Schuster Speakers Bureau at 1-866-248-3049 or visit our website at www.simonspeakers.com.

Interior design by Michelle Kelly
Image © 123RF

Manufactured in the United States of America

1 2023

Library of Congress Cataloging-in-Publication Data
Names: Mahler, Jaime, author.
Title: Toxic relationship recovery / Jaime Mahler, MS, LMHC.
Description: First Adams Media trade paperback edition | Stoughton, Massachusetts: Adams Media, [2023] | Includes bibliographical references and index.
Identifiers: LCCN 2023016624 | ISBN 9781507220504 (pb) | ISBN 9781507220511 (ebook)
Subjects: LCSH: Interpersonal relations--Psychological aspects. | Interpersonal conflict. | Classification: LCC HM1106 .M337 2023 | DDC 302--dc23/eng/20230411
LC record available at https://lccn.loc.gov/2023016624

ISBN 978-1-5072-2050-4
ISBN 978-1-5072-2051-1 (ebook)

# CONTENTS

# DEDICATION

To my cherished partner, Stewart
My vibrant children, Caden, Theo, and Azelee,
and to my most beloved friend CA

# ACKNOWLEDGMENTS

This book would not have been possible without every single one of you. The reason this book was able to come to fruition was the passion of the people that care about recovering from toxic relationships, harmful narratives, and complex trauma. Thank you for your continued interest in my social media platforms and commitment to unlearning generational trauma.

I'd also like to thank my editing team at Simon & Schuster, especially Leah D'Sa and Laura Daly, for rooting for me during many setbacks while writing this book. I'm thankful to Adams Media for believing in the power of this book and believing in me.

I want to thank my large family in New York and my extended family all over the country who cheered me on throughout this past year. I want to thank Kimberly, who inspired me to take the leap and become a therapist as well as start posting on social media. I want to thank CA, who stayed with me through the hardest parts of this year and passionately spoke truth into my life when I didn't believe in myself.

My children, Caden, Theo, and Azelee, inspire me to challenge past narratives that I was taught and to fight to create a world for them that is less cruel and more psychologically safe. My hope is that you all can find partners who enrich your lives the way your father enriches mine. But, even more than that, I hope you will grow up to love yourselves, deeply, with a kindness and compassion that comes from knowing you are incredibly worthy and incredibly valuable.

Lastly, I want to thank my partner, Stewart, who took on a lot of extra work and tasks while I wrote this book. He has journeyed with me through some of my darkest days. Stewart, thank you for seeing me when I couldn't see myself. Thank you for giving me the space I needed to sort through my own toxicity. Thank you for allowing me to catch up to you when I stumbled far behind. Thank you for showing me what a real and healthy relationship can look like. Thank you for knowing I was capable of becoming who I am today. I love you.

# INTRODUCTION

A toxic relationship is any connection with another person that makes you feel devalued, attacked, or neglected. This dynamic can occur in any type of relationship, but this book will focus on intimate relationships. Romantic bonds that are toxic are heartbreaking, confusing, traumatic, and very difficult to disentangle yourself from. But there *is* a way out and forward. With *Toxic Relationship Recovery: Your Guide to Identifying Toxic Partners, Leaving Unhealthy Dynamics, and Healing Emotional Wounds after a Breakup*, you'll learn how to let go of your toxic partner, understand what you went through, mend invisible wounds, and set healthy standards for future relationships. Even if you feel angry, sad, terrified, or hopeless right now, you can unearth a world beyond this pain.

Maybe you've noticed the red flags in your toxic relationship: your partner's constant criticism, gaslighting, refusal to accept responsibility, or emotional and/or physical abuse. These and other factors create a very unhealthy relationship dynamic that is hard to live with but can be even harder to leave. Whether you've already ended your relationship, or you think it might be time to end it, this book can guide you gently in the right direction.

This book is divided into two parts. In Part 1: Understanding Your Relationship with Them, you'll learn exactly what makes a modern relationship toxic, how it can get that way, and how to recognize and accept what happened so you can avoid those circumstances going forward. Then in Part 2: Healing Your Relationship with Yourself, you'll work on skills and strategies that focus on healing wounds that continue to hurt after the relationship is over; you'll reaffirm your identity outside of this relationship and discover how to truly be happy again. Throughout the book, you'll find real-world examples of common situations that might resonate with you and you'll complete simple exercises that allow you to put your newfound knowledge into action right away. Each chapter ends with key take-aways you can refer back to as you evolve and grow.

Know that you are not alone in this struggle—and that you can move past this trauma into a new phase of your life. Take control of your situation, reclaim your power, and look ahead with pride, deter-mination, and optimism. Whether you're looking for a healthy, loving relationship or some peaceful time to enjoy your own company, let *Toxic Relationship Recovery* help you build the life you deserve.

**PART 1**

# UNDERSTANDING YOUR RELATIONSHIP WITH THEM

In Part 1, you will be exploring the true evolution and definition of a toxic relationship. Each chapter walks through both parties' perspectives so you can gain a deep understanding of how this situation evolves into a vicious perpetual loop. Even though this material is difficult to read, take a moment and have courage. You don't get to choose your foundations, but you are now the captain and the navigator of your journey. You now can speak your own truth over the lies and unhealthy examples that have been provided for you in the past.

Though every toxic relationship is unique to some extent, they all have common traits that help define them. Unhealthy habits like love-bombing and gaslighting take hold, and trauma continues through methods of control or emotional neglect. Many toxic relationships also involve codependency or other types of unhealthy attachment. These issues often lead to a breakup cycle where a breakup happens, self-doubt and false narratives creep in, and then the person returns to the toxic relationship. Understanding your relationship with them will help you identify which topics will be useful to focus on during your recovery.

# CHAPTER 1

# EXAMINING HOW RELATIONSHIPS WERE MODELED FOR YOU

Consider all the relationships in your life for a moment. You began your life with a relationship with one or both parents. You learned to relate to your siblings and peers. Eventually you learned to relate to others through media and possibly through the lens of faith as well. Every single relationship you engaged in slowly built a foundation for what you expect in a relationship. You learned how to think and act in relationships. You learned relationship "norms." You learned from modeling the behaviors of others and observing and trying out different strategies you witnessed.

The journey to healing and moving forward from toxic relationships starts with looking at your early relationships and tracing where your own foundational constructs around relationships began. Examining these family, friend, media, and spiritual foundations will shed light on the things that need to be unlearned in order to promote healthier connections. This chapter will be challenging your perceptions of yourself and your relationships. You will be asked to step back and review how you have conceptualized relationships in each part of your life, and why and how those beliefs led you to where you are right now.

# THE FAMILY FOUNDATION

We all yearn for connection, beginning at a young age. Within the family system, everyone wants to be noticed, to be included, and to be cared for.

In fact, the first place most people develop their beliefs about love is within their family. At the same time that children need connection and community, they also have a need for individuality. Within the family system, there is a balancing act between these different, yet equally important, elements of a relationship—one that will continue to influence you as you grow up and form adult connections. Many other factors come into play as you learn how to relate to others—for example, the behavior your parents modeled for you, the concept of being authentic versus denying who you are, the extra connections present in sibling relationships, can create foundational confusion. In the sections that follow, you will explore each of these key parts of the family foundation in more detail.

## THE NEED FOR INDIVIDUALITY

The dichotomy that occurs in relationships with others is that people have an intense need for love and belonging that coexists with an intense need for autonomy and individuality. This need is typically stifled when we are young. Children are constantly told things like, "You are part of a team," "You are part of this classroom," "You are part of this family," and/or "You are part of this church," and the caregivers fail to mention the importance of the child's need for individuality. Children don't typically hear: "You are an individual." Yes, it is important for children to learn how to share and be in community with others. Yet, at the same time, children need to be able to foster their individuality.

People who were discouraged to be individuals often later end up feeling guilt or shame in situations where they attempt to advocate for that individuality. Small moments that may have seemed like nothing when you were a child can start to build deeper beliefs and behaviors that stifle your individuality. This can look like having to wear matching outfits, you and your sibling being forced to do the same sport, or not being allowed to play alone. You may have been forced to share everything: a room, your birthday toys, your music, your clothes. In a situation where individuality is being discouraged, externally the child gets shamed for asking for their own clothes or their own identity and internally feels guilty for having those needs.

---

### Case Study:
### Challenges with Individuality and Siblings

Sara is ten years old. She has a close relationship with her sister, Gia, who is eight years old. Gia looks up to Sara and, at times, she follows her around the house waiting for Sara to come up with something for both of them to do. While Sara loves to feel needed, at times she struggles with finding the balance between Gia's needs and wanting time for herself. She initially is excited when Gia asks her to plan out their morning together, yet an hour into playing outside, she gets frustrated when Gia continually asks her, "What's next?" Sara, frustrated, turns to Gia and says, "Ugh, you are so annoying, leave me alone!" Gia is confused; she starts tearing up and runs inside. Sara feels both guilt and relief watching her sister go inside.

Gia received a message that was very confusing. She saw Sara being excited about spending time together, then there was a sudden emotional switch from Sara that left Gia unsure of what she did wrong.

---

There is nothing wrong with wanting to belong and be in connection with another person. There is also nothing wrong with needing time to yourself. The issue becomes when skills in communication, emotional processing, and empathy are lacking. Unfortunately, these are skills many children are never taught.

Understanding that you may have not had the skills to identify and articulate what was going on with you emotionally as a child will help you start processing and healing some of the wounds that may have been developed from this lack of individual expression. If you have difficulty expressing your personal needs now as an adult, examine whether any of that reluctance might have originated in your childhood.

## What Is Emotional Processing?

Emotional processing is a method of reflection and introspection that helps you transform an emotional experience or feeling into useful information for your psyche to consider. When applied to your healing process and filtered through a healthy lens, this information can provide the stabilization you'll need to move forward in your recovery.

## ALL-OR-NOTHING VERSUS BOTH/AND THINKING

A child who has experienced this tug of war between their desire for individuality and the external demand for community may become confused. They are being given the message that their need for individuality is selfish. But they crave that room to grow on their own so much—how could such a deep-rooted need be unacceptable?

Here's an idea that seems simple but can be revolutionary when you feel this confusion: Two emotions can coexist and be equally valid. This is a blending of two emotions in one psychological space. Processing two emotions at once is called *both/and* processing. Picture yourself as a child processing this thought: *I know I love my sister but I also know it's important for me to have alone time.* Now imagine changing the "but" to an "and." You are allowed to feel both love and frustration at the same time in this situation, yet the skills necessary to do this are not typically taught to most children.

Instead, most people are taught *all-or-nothing* thinking. Usually, what children are told is: "You either include your sister (*all*) or you're saying you don't care about her (*nothing*)." This encourages the child to choose their sister's needs over their own needs. The child becomes confused because the psyche longs to fulfill *both* needs—we can call this a both/and mindset.

In intimate partnerships, this kind of confusion, if constant, is something to pay closer attention to. Feeling bad about having or expressing your needs, feeling like your partner takes more than they give, receiving mixed messages about how to please them, feeling as though regardless of what you do your partner is never satisfied—this is all confusion that stems from the foundations built during your early development.

All-or-nothing thinking is a cognitive distortion that was identified and popularized by David Burns in his book *Feeling Good: The New Mood Therapy*. Burns describes all-or-nothing thinking as a tendency to think in extremes. All-or-nothing thinking is a distorted filter the brain runs information through. It is a story that says when you are processing an emotion, there is no middle ground. For example, if your adult sister disappointed you by not showing up to your birthday party, the all-or-nothing narrative says, "She doesn't care about you; she doesn't value you at all." In other words, it's the extreme best- or worst-case scenario and there is no possibility for an in-between interpretation. In this case, maybe your sister did not have time to call you to tell you that one of her kids got sick and she couldn't make it. All-or-nothing thinking is a distorted thought pattern. The both/and skill is a direct counter to the all-or-nothing pattern.

## Thematic Depth

While you are exploring the concepts discussed in this book, try to focus on the thematic depth of the issue. *Thematic depth* refers to finding a deeper understanding about yourself or certain issues. *Thematic* refers to pulling out the themes of what seems to be a surface-level issue—for example, shame, rejection, confusion, or people pleasing, to name a few. *Depth* refers to the process of pulling out purpose, reason, value, and information about that issue that you didn't previously see by just glancing at the surface. When you explore the thematic depth of a situation, you're asking yourself for the complex underlying details of the situation.

## PARENTIFICATION

Parentification is treating a child like an adult throughout their childhood. It is very harmful to the psyche because it teaches the child to first and foremost anticipate their parents' needs. When the child becomes an adult, the adult then enters into intimate partnerships in which they continue to prioritize their partner's needs. Many parentified children show up to adulthood as people pleasers, perfectionists, peacekeepers, and problem solvers. Unfortunately, these attributes come at the expense of their own development and growth. Adults who were parentified as children typically take on other people's responsibilities because that is what was modeled to them as normal. They struggle with differentiating their own needs from the responsibilities and obligations of others.

## ENMESHMENT

Enmeshment occurs when any relationship (family or otherwise) has either poor boundaries or no boundaries. The concept of enmeshment was first introduced by the psychotherapist Salvador Minuchin, who described enmeshed families as characterized by a high level of communication but low levels of healthy distance and individual differentiation. People in enmeshed relationships see personal boundaries and personal autonomy as a threat to the integrity of the relationship.

An enmeshed family is one in which everybody knows everything about everyone. Gossip runs rampant because it's a given that the family needs to be updated constantly about *every* life event that anyone has. Family functions reign supreme. Every family member is expected to show up at every holiday, every birthday, every gathering, and if one person does not appear (possibly because they are attending to their own needs) that absence is looked at as selfish, disrespectful, and rude.

## PARENT "NORMS"

Beyond what they teach you about individuality, your family also paves the way for the relationship models you cultivate, through the example they set. Whether you grew up with a single parent, two parents, blended family, or other situation, by witnessing your parents interact with each other and everyday life, you learned an immense amount of information—and determined what you thought of as "normal." Your parents taught you what to tolerate, what to consent to, what to endure, how to approach suffering, and how to interact with emotions, all through their own example. They also taught you what to do when life gets hard and what to do when a loved one hurts you. Children learn a lot as they watch their caregivers go through situations and observe how they manage, avoid, or disengage from issues.

*Whether you grew up with a single parent, two parents, blended family, or other situation, by witnessing your parents interact with each other and everyday life, you learned an immense amount of information—and determined what you thought of as "normal."*

An often-overlooked learning model in childhood development is learning by omission. Learning by omission is when someone doesn't process a stressor or doesn't engage in a conversation about a difficult topic. Children draw conclusions around disengagement from this example as well. Imagine that you are a child who told your parent about someone bullying you at school and they just shrug it off. From this experience, you learn that not only does your parent not offer real solutions for you in your time of need, but also that they will disengage from the problem and may even make you feel silly for bringing it up. If this dynamic continues through childhood, the child quickly learns that their needs are unimportant, their self-advocacy is futile, and that when they encounter an overwhelming situation, they are completely on their own to handle it.

This kind of foundation impacts not only your family relationships, but your future intimate relationships as well. You may see this later in life show up as a tendency to self-isolate when you are overwhelmed or try to manage a tough situation entirely on your own without asking for any help.

## Case Study: Perpetuating Norms

Jay is sixteen; he is just starting to explore his feelings for girls and he is watching a few of his peers explore relationships with girls. He was raised primarily by his mother, with his father there for dinners and yard work on the weekends but not emotionally present. Jay's mom stayed at home but constantly bypassed her own parental authority, always telling Jay and his older brothers to "ask Dad" about any decision that needed to be made. As a result, Jay and his brothers do not see their mother as confident or capable.

Jay's older brothers have already started dating and regularly speak in a derogatory way about the girls in their school, as well as criticizing their girlfriends for not "putting out" when they want them to. Through his brothers, Jay is learning a "norm" that says it is the girlfriend's responsibility to acquiesce to any demands that her boyfriend may have around sex.

Jay starts talking to a girl in his class, and they begin dating. Jay immediately starts bypassing his new girlfriend's decisions, citing that he is the man in the relationship and this is just how it is. He also pesters his girlfriend about not meeting his physical needs and implies that this is primarily his girlfriend's responsibility in the relationship.

Consider how these narratives might play out if they were left unchallenged and unchecked into adulthood. Jay is normalizing that a woman should be at his beck and call and his family is reinforcing that narrative. This situation builds a strong belief system that allows him to tell himself that he is right to be the one to make these demands, and that any woman who doesn't follow his demands or cater to his needs is lazy, bossy, or a prude.

## AUTHENTICITY VERSUS DENIAL

Having successful relationships truly starts with being authentic. If your parents struggled with being honest with themselves and chose the passive-aggressive route when encountering a difficult issue, or just chose sheer denial when someone blatantly called them out, you likely caught on quickly that your parents refused to be held accountable for their actions or the way they hurt you.

If you talked to your parent about the bullying situation and told them, "Listen, it really hurt me when you shrugged off that situation with the bully the other day," and they replied, "I don't know what you're talking about," they utilized denial in order to not be held accountable for their behavior. When you get older, you may struggle with holding yourself accountable for situations, which would align with what you were modeled growing up. You could also, however, swing the pendulum the other way and take accountability for things that aren't your responsibility to begin with. You can see it clearly play out in this example:

**You:** I'm not sure if you forgot, but my birthday was yesterday.

**Your Partner:** Well, you should have reminded me!

**You:** You are right, I will remind you next year.

In this scenario, your partner remained fixed in denying a basic responsibility of a partnership. If your partner and you celebrate birthdays, it is reasonable to expect your partner to remember that day on their own without a reminder. If you take on the full responsibility of the situation, your partner remains complacent in their lack of attunement to the relationship needs and you become fully responsible for their lack of thoughtfulness.

## Exercise: Examine Your Family Foundations

Now that you have explored different relationship foundations created within a family and how they impact your later relationships, take a moment to think about your own childhood relationship dynamics.

Go through this list and do your best to answer each question with radical honesty:

- Was there ever a time when you felt responsible for other people's happiness? If yes, describe a specific example.
- Was there ever a time when you felt guilty for asking for your individual time and space? If yes, describe a specific example.
- What, if any, intense negative emotions (for example, shame, guilt, anger, fear) do you remember feeling in your childhood in relation with others?
- Consider the emotional themes of your childhood. Can you identify any themes related to, for example, feeling left out, people pleasing, or frustration?
- Using your answers to the previous questions, identify different norms that were established in your family and write them down.

Emotions carry a lot of insight into the things that affect us, and what weight we carry from childhood into our adult lives. Exploring your emotions can help you recognize family norms that you may have ignored or viewed as "the way it is for everyone" in the past.

# THE FRIEND FOUNDATION

The next influence on your beliefs and behaviors in intimate relationships is your friends and peer groups. Friends are highly valued—at times valued even higher than your siblings or parents. The way friends act in relationships, especially in the early teen years, can inform what you think of as normal.

## HOW TOXICITY CAN ENTER

Let's break down how toxicity can become normalized in a friend group. When a person starts treating their partner poorly, the friend group that is aware of that behavior has a choice. The friend group can either address the poor treatment, stay silent (this is typically perceived as a neutral position), or encourage the maltreatment. If the friend group stays silent or encourages the behavior, it creates a norm. This norm allows the person to say, "In that friend group, I can treat my partner badly and my friends will not 'check' my behavior or may encourage me to continue to mistreat my partner." The more this is touted as an acceptable behavior, the more it becomes the norm. For example, if all of your friends lie to their partners, then it becomes more acceptable for you to lie to your partner.

## Exercise: Reflect On Your Friendship Foundations

Peer relationship norms can be very influential to your development of relationship norms, so take a moment to review what is considered normal in your peer groups, either now or in key moments in your childhood. Your answers will guide you in the Practice Radical Self-Honesty exercise at the end of this chapter as well.

- First, reflect on the friends that seem to be rejected by your group. Why are they outcast? What about them is being singled out as a reason for the group to spurn them? Consider why, as sometimes happens, the friend group continues to foster a connection with an identified outcast and what utility having that person around serves. Is the outcasted friend invited to gatherings so there is someone to bully? Are they invited because the friend group lacks direct communication skills to clarify that they are not connecting as friends anymore?
- Now consider the friend who shows up authentically. Is authenticity common in your friend group? Is there one person who seems to bring a sense of much-needed clarity to the group?
- Ask yourself how these authentic friends are received by others in the group. Are they ostracized for not going along with the "groupthink" of their peers? Are they listened to or viewed as a source of good advice?
- What behaviors are encouraged by your friends, either by laughing or cheering them on, and what behaviors are discouraged by your friends, either by bullying them or emotionally neglecting them and leaving them out?

It's easy to feel pressured or encouraged when in a group of your peers to do something you might not want to do or that you might otherwise find harmful. The norms established with friends can sometimes be healthy and nurturing, or they can perpetuate toxic relationship norms.

## THE FAITH FOUNDATION

This topic will not be applicable to all, but it's worth noting as many folks have been raised in religious households. If religious ideologies were placed at a high priority in your family, certain religion-specific relationship norms may have been taught and reinforced throughout your upbringing.

Religious norms that influence beliefs about relationships might include:

- How different genders are supposed to act.
- What occupations different genders should have.
- What financial responsibilities each gender should have.
- Who is the leader of the relationship.
- Whether relationship roles are equitable.
- What role submission plays in the relationship and whether that submission is consensual.
- What the role of sex is in the relationship and the consent expectations around sex.
- The roles of each parent in a family.
- How children should be raised, encouraged, disciplined, educated, etc.

Religious norms can lay a foundation that creates a deep sense of self within a relationship. For those who believe in the narrative that the religion teaches, that can be very meaningful, and will play an important role in the values prioritized in their relationships. However, if you questioned religious beliefs in any way, you may have experienced tension with family members—even a feeling that you were not accepted.

Naturally, as a child it's easier to go along with the narrative of your family. But as you get older, your own beliefs start to emerge, and they may not always line up with the beliefs of others in your community. Guilt and shame are typically present when this occurs because developing unique ideas can often be framed as turning your back on the family/religious community you are in. It is necessary to reflect on where your religious upbringing and your authentic self intersect—or don't.

## Exercise: Describe Your Religious Foundations

Using the list of religion-related relationship norms provided in this section of the chapter, answer the following questions:

- What religious norms did you grow up learning and practicing?
- Which of these norms feel authentic to you?
- Which of these norms feel imposed on you, or just don't resonate with your adult beliefs?

By determining which values are authentic to you, you can better understand what is important to you in intimate relationships, and what norms may be getting in the way of healthy connections.

## THE MEDIA FOUNDATION

Regardless of what generation you grew up in, it's safe to say you were exposed to relationship norms on TV, the Internet, and/or your smartphone. Whether it was Lucy and Ricky on *I Love Lucy*, Ross and Rachel on *Friends*, Cam and Mitchell on *Modern Family*, or a real-life couple playing out their relationship on *Instagram*, the norms you are exposed to through the media can affect how you think about and act in your own relationships. Because we can invest hours upon hours getting to know these characters and social media personalities and feeling emotionally connected to them, it would be remiss to not explore how the media can skew our definition of a normal relationship.

# Exercise: Determine How the Media Impacted Your Perception of Relationships

As you reflect on your media foundations—what you watched or read about the most—answer the following questions:

- What type of media did you consume the most when you were younger?
- What relationships were memorable for you in that media?
- What themes did those relationships model to you (for example, on-again/off-again, betrayal/cheating, lying to get out of things, passive aggression, revenge)?
- What themes that you just identified are also found in your relationships today (keep in mind this can be any relationship: family, friend, partner)?

## WHAT DID A "TYPICAL" RELATIONSHIP LOOK LIKE TO YOU?

The media models what "typical" relationships look like. *Typical* is in quotations here because media depictions of relationships are anything but normal. We see exaggerations of overinflated love. We see wild expressions of romance. We see vicious fights and tumultuous affairs as a part of what it means to truly love someone. What is important to note here is that if a show or celebrity news focused on calm, reasonable love, we would be bored. If we saw two adults dialoguing through a conflict, we would be bored. Two adults listening and honoring each other's pain is a lot less interesting than a blowout argument. So, what we get in our newsfeed and what streaming services offer is what boosts ratings and keeps us engaged: chaos, treachery, backstabbing, confusion, jealousy, and whirlwind ravenous romance. Authentic love isn't entertaining to watch. It's not fueled by pain and lust. Yes, it has its ups and downs, but it is not driven by chaos, and it can honestly be boring sometimes. Love does not necessarily equal trauma and drama; you might have to unlearn a few things related to that fact if media norms have impacted your views on relationships.

## Exercise: Identify Your Relationship Norms

Now that you have explored the different foundations and norms that can affect your beliefs about relationships, let's use the answers in the previous exercises to piece together a bigger picture of the foundations that are impactful for you.

- What do you consider to be relationship "norms"?
- What foundations did those ideas come from?
- Break down specific ways each foundation—family, friends, faith, media—influenced your beliefs about relationships. Which foundation do you consider to be the most influential?
- What elements did/do your most recent relationship have that are "norms" but may not actually be normal or healthy?
- What elements would you say are found in a healthy relationship? Which of these elements were present in your most recent/current relationship and which elements were absent?
- What internal narratives (ideas/voices) come into your mind when you consider if it's possible for you to actually have a healthy relationship? (For example, *That's nice, but that is just for fairytales; That type of respect isn't real; Why would anyone want to be with me if I'm damaged?;* etc.)

It's very important that you do this exercise right now because the answers will serve as a reference point as you go through this book. You will be able to look back at what you thought was normal, acceptable, and healthy and see just how far you've come.

## YOUR BASELINE RELATIONSHIP SKILLS

You've learned about what things are present in a toxic foundation. Now, as you reflect on and process how these pillars have impacted you, you may recognize something that is *missing* in toxic foundations: relationship skills. Healthy relationship skills such as communication skills, emotional processing skills, compassion and empathy skills, and tuning into your authenticity are crucial to creating and maintaining a deeply meaningful and thriving relationship. And if your sphere of influence did not have the skills to establish healthy relationships in their own lives, how were you supposed to learn these skills yourself? If you did not have any models for healthy relationship building, it will be no surprise if these skills do not manifest when you begin to explore your own intimate partnerships as an adult. Fortunately, these skills can be built at any time in order to heal from relational trauma and promote healthy future connections; it all starts with an awareness that something isn't normal, learning from harmful skills, and practicing radical self-honesty.

## What Is Relational Trauma?

Relational trauma is trauma that occurs within the interpersonal dynamic between two people. This is trauma *in* the connection. Trauma itself is simply anything that disrupts the core concept of who you are and shakes or violates the values that you have deep within you. Let's say you have a strong value system around dressing nicely when you go out. Relational trauma might look like your partner saying sharply, "Who are you dressing up for?!" You are confused and explain to them, "I always wear this kind of outfit when I go out; it makes me happy!" They reply, "Take it off! Stop begging for attention; it's pathetic!"

At first glance someone might question if relational trauma is occurring here, but let's break this down together. A person has a value system around their personal expression of self. They already did the reflective work and found a system that resonates with them (this could be anything—fashion, makeup, working out). In this case, the expression was clothes. The partner not only asserted their opinion over their partner's but also then denigrated them and inserted their own narrative over the whole experience. Now, take that one experience and multiply it by ten, twenty, a hundred? That is complex relational trauma because it is prolonged and persistent. We will discuss complex trauma more in Chapter 3, but for now understand that relational trauma can be a one-time occurrence, or it can happen in small incremental ways every day in a relationship. Either way, its impact is devastating to the psyche.

## THAT'S NOT NORMAL

Being able to say "that's not normal" is a powerful thing. The process of unlearning starts with gaining this knowledge and awareness. Being able to identify a relationship norm that you once thought was normal and calling it what it truly is (toxic), is a turning point for you. As you get deeper into this book, you will be learning new and healthy ways to navigate your relationships and heal from toxic bonds—and it starts with saying out loud, "You know what, that was not normal. It was toxic, and it caused me immense pain."

## CREATING THE NEW BY LEARNING FROM THE OLD

If you have relational skills but those skills were modeled to you by a toxic relationship, they can be malicious skills, like manipulation, passive aggression, deception, harmful physical coping strategies (throwing, punching, and/or breaking things); you may also have learned harmful emotional coping strategies (complete silent treatment, pretending nothing happened, distracting the pain away, suppressing authentic emotion and emotional pain). By evaluating the skills that were modeled to you, you can start to develop a framework for what skills are truly useful to nurturing healthy, happy bonds, and what skills continue or enable toxic relational patterns. Harmful skills give you new information for growth.

## USING RADICAL SELF-HONESTY AS YOU REFLECT

Radical self-honesty is a practice that you will encounter throughout this book. It is the practice of connecting with the authentic reason you employed a certain defense mechanism or trauma-informed skill, disengaged from a situation, or engaged in any other potentially harmful behavior. It is about connecting with the authentic thoughts and feelings behind a behavior and being truthful toward yourself so you can use that information to move forward in a healthier way. Radical self-honesty looks like asking yourself, *Why do I really want to text them back?* Then processing all the authentic thoughts and emotions behind that impulse to text. Perhaps the reason you want to text back is because you are lonely and want someone—anyone—to keep you company, even if that company hurts you. While practicing this radical self-honesty you would then dig deeper into why it's so easy for you to reengage with a partner who hurts you so badly. You would ask yourself the hard questions like, *Why do I find it so easy to betray myself when I am lonely?* Radical self-honesty can be uncomfortable and many times painful; however, it is also powerful. When you are radically self-honest you are dropping the previous "truths" that you were taught and listening deep within. Listen for that poignant wisdom that exists within you.

## Exercise: Practice Radical Self-Honesty

This exercise will help you start honing your skills in radical self-honesty. To begin, think back to a moment you felt emotional dissonance—meaning, a difference between something that was normalized for you and the deeper truth. For example, maybe there was a time when you thought it was acceptable for a partner to insult you in front of your friends. Use radical self-honesty as you answer these questions to reflect on a specific situation that you went through:

- Think of a specific situation that you suspect you normalized in the past. This situation must be a time during which you felt a lot of psychological tension and frustration.
- Think about the situation and the tension that occurred. What did you do in your mind with that dissonance? Where did the energy go?
- If you dismissed that dissonance, how did you dismiss it? Name the thoughts (for example: *Forget about it*; *Ugh, whatever*).
- If you distracted yourself, name your go-to distractions. (Keep in mind that people, relationships, and work can be distractions.)
- If you processed the dissonance, how did you go about processing it?

It's important here to not only acknowledge dissonance, but to also learn to hold it, honor it with a pause, and practice better processing it to tune into your most authentic self.

## HOW TRAUMA SKEWS RELATIONSHIP NEEDS

Before closing this chapter, it's important to give some attention to what can so often be forgotten, especially when caught up in a toxic relationship: your needs. Everyone has unique needs for their relationship. Some may say to this, "But I didn't have needs when I went into the relationship." However, even if you have not established any overt needs, there are things you deserve in a relationship. You deserve basic human decency. You deserve to be in a relationship that feels safe. You deserve kindness, gentleness, and compassion. You deserve to be heard and understood. Ignoring your needs is part of the toxic dynamic. If you don't have any needs (that you are aware of), then your partner doesn't have to show up in any particular way. They can do the bare minimum of what is expected of a partner and that is seen as normal and healthy.

If you had needs that were founded on trauma or modeled after toxic relationships, anyone who meets those needs isn't looked at as the problem. You had needs; they met them. So if you're accused of "making a fuss" or "being dramatic," when you are actually just trying to process the harm they are causing or challenge the cycle of conflict you find yourself in, it's now pushed back onto you as your fault and you accept that as truth.

It's easy to accept this "truth" because you may have realized that because you never articulated your need for basic human decency, asking for it now can feel like "too much." The more you are convinced you are asking for too much, the more this relationship will feel like it's anchored on you just keeping the peace and not ruffling your partner's feathers, setting aside your needs. It bears repeating: You deserve basic human decency. And you shouldn't have to ask for it. Of course, because toxic relationships can twist the truth and have you question whether your basic need for respect is too much, it can feel uncomfortable to sit with the radical idea that you deserve kindness. So if you haven't heard this in a while, pause to internalize it now: You have value.

You don't have to prove you are valuable, or earn your value. You are worthy *now*. Carry this knowledge with you as you continue through this book.

## KEY TAKEAWAYS

- The relationships that surrounded you as a child (your sphere of influence) were critical foundations in the development of what you consider to be "normal" in any relationship.
- By identifying both helpful and harmful relationship skills that were modeled for you during your development, you can now begin to break the toxic relationship cycle.
- The all-or-nothing narrative must be identified in emotional processing in order to unlearn it; without reflection it looks like a normal mindset.
- The both/and mentality provides a direct counter skill to the all-or-nothing narrative.
- Radical self-honesty is a fundamental emotional processing skill that creates the foundation for the authentic self.
- You are worthy of kindness, safety, and respect. Basic human decency is your right.

# CHAPTER 2

# COMMON PATTERNS IN TOXIC RELATIONSHIPS

The factors present in a toxic relationship can help identify issues that you need to process as you heal from the relationship. In this chapter, we will be focusing on key elements such as your partner's fundamental personality traits and typical ways of addressing conflict. Analyzing these factors will deepen your understanding of the components of toxic relationships and how to avoid them in the future. At first glance, you may not think it's important to dive into the past—and it may feel painful to do so—but this process can lead to healing.

## UNDERSTANDING EMOTIONALLY UNSKILLED PARTNERS

A common component of partners with toxic behaviors is that they are emotionally unskilled. Emotionally unskilled partners struggle to identify their emotions, to process those emotions, and to understand the implications of their behaviors. Because they lack these skills, their behavior in relationships can be very harmful and toxic. A key point, though: Most of the time an emotionally unskilled partner is showing up that way *unintentionally*. The sad part about many toxic relationships is that your partner may have never intended to hurt you at all. Unfortunately, they joined the relationship unformed, unhealed, and/or unskilled in the tools necessary to make a healthy partnership. The partner who is lacking skills can either realize they need to develop emotional navigation skills or they can shrug and say, "This is just who I am."

If you find yourself in a relationship with someone who has very few relational skills, it may seem normal to you; perhaps while you were growing up, many of the adults around you also lacked relational skills. They may not have:

- Modeled how to identify emotions.
- Shared or processed their feelings, so they instead continued traumatic patterns.
- Shown you what true accountability and acknowledgment of their actions looked like.

Even if you have done the work to develop your relationship skills and are ready now as an adult to begin to create a healthy partnership, your partner's lack of skill can become a barrier to your own personal growth as well as a barrier to the growth of the relationship. When even one partner remains unskilled, it can become a big problem.

## IS IT UNINTENTIONAL OR INTENTIONAL MANIPULATION?

So many partners who are seeking healing from harmful relationships ask me, Does my partner mean to be this manipulative? Do you think they knew how harmful they were? Do you think they even realized how they were being coercive? It's tough to answer these questions in a clear-cut way because even though most people aren't intentionally manipulative, their continued lack of emotional skills makes them seem like they are.

Partners who unintentionally manipulate can still be very difficult to problem-solve with because their lack of awareness fuels their belief that they are blameless. If one partner believes the best way to solve a problem is to ignore it, and the other partner points out that by ignoring the issue they are neglecting the relationship, they won't get past square one. This is where perception is everything. When a partner is willing to at least understand that their actions have implications to the world around them, they can gain awareness of how those behaviors radically affect others. Assuming they care about how their behavior affects others, this awareness is the beginning of their true transformation. If, on the other hand, the partner realizes their behavior affects others but continues to refuse to gain the necessary skills it takes to maintain a healthy relationship, they are making a choice not to grow. If they then give lip service to their partner and say, "I get it, I hurt you," but do not change their behavior, that is intentionally manipulative.

The partner who is attempting to call out the issues that need to be worked on now often feels confused. They realize that the first step to healing is education and awareness, and they see that their partner seems to be at that stage of healing—yet they have made no progress. The person who does not develop relational skills and stops at "awareness" is essentially leading their partner on and being intentionally manipulative. They are "appeasing teasing." They know if they acknowledge there is an issue but do nothing to work on resolving the issue, they can barely lift a finger and come off as though they are doing enough work for the relationship. In fact, the real work of relationships happens *after* awareness. The real work of relationships is found within the actions and reactions of the dynamic.

## TYPES OF TOXIC PARTNERS

Everyone wants to give a good first impression, and you probably were drawn to some of your partner's more enticing qualities at first. In toxic relationships, however, your first few interactions with your partner can also expose traits that will become more problematic later. In fact, if you look back at the way a toxic partner showed up initially, you will probably see that they gave you the exact information that would predict that the relationship would become toxic. Following are a few common types of toxic partners and how they present themselves at first.

## THE DISTRESSED

Their motto: "Save Me."

Their main need: To be helped.

Traits that draw people to them:

- They ask for help.
- They will make you feel important.
- They will make you feel needed.
- They might idolize you or put you on a pedestal.
- They will bond with you quickly.

The Distressed partner may look like they are falling apart, but when they explain to you that all they need is love in order to be whole again, it's easy to fall for them. The Distressed partner attracts people who like to "fix" problems. After all, what's better than feeling needed? Sometimes people confuse those two feelings, however: Do you really love this person, or do you just love to feel needed?

The Distressed partner is also an attractive match for people who are fulfilled by helping others. The Distressed partner wants to be "saved," which might look like depending on you for car payments, grocery money (even when you don't live together), or assistance with school or work demands. These relationships become codependent very fast.

## THE CATCH

Their motto: "Capture Me."

Their main need: To be admired.

Traits that draw people to them:

- They may be successful.
- They may have money or status.
- They may have their life "put together" (a job, a home, a car).
- They may be charming or popular.
- They may be physically attractive.

The Catch is someone who knows they have something highly coveted. Maybe they are super attractive, or maybe they have great hair, fashionable clothes, or a lot of money. Maybe they are a local celebrity or hold a special place of honor in their town, or maybe they are in a position of power, such as a police officer, politician, doctor, business owner, or professor. If you are able to capture the Catch, it can feel like a real honor and can make you feel like a local celebrity as well.

Because of their power, at any moment the Catch could be snatched away from you. The Catch is aware of this power, and looks for a partner who is attracted to success. They hope that their success will help you overlook some of the red flags they possess, excuse their lack of relationship skills, and justify their harmful relationship tactics such as invalidating your successes, constantly comparing you to them, ignoring your needs (because their dreams are more important), or throwing money at problems instead of working on them.

## THE HUNTER

Their motto: "Submit to Me."

Their main need: To maintain power.

Traits that draw people to them:

- They come off as powerful (but the power comes from exploiting other people).
- They come off as confident (but this is actually disguised arrogance).
- They come off as ambitious (but the ambition is unbalanced and often merely stubbornness).

The Hunter consciously seeks a particular type of partner dictated by their patriarchal system, religious group, or politically affiliated family. The type may vary, but some common examples of this are a man looking for a submissive wife—someone who will obey him, dress a certain way, and/or not challenge him in any way. Another example might be a powerful political family who is looking for a man to marry into their family who shares the same beliefs as them and doesn't have any "new ideas" that could shake things up. It can feel like a privilege if a Hunter decides you meet their lofty standards.

Hunters are particular about the person they want to match up with, not because of a personal preference, but to maintain a sense of power over the relationship or a sense of power over the narrative of the relationship. They aren't looking for a partner who has individual opinions, individual autonomy, or an individualistic approach to life. The Hunter will seek out a person who is either indifferent or submissive and is actively exhibiting attributes that align with the maintenance of the Hunter's power. The Hunter can be incredibly toxic since the primary motivator or reason the relationship exists in the first place is because of power or their perception of power.

## THE USER

Their motto: "Elevate Me."
Their main need: To raise their status.
Traits that draw people to them:
  • They are committed to the relationship.

The User is looking for someone to elevate them in some way, such as financially, in terms of power or name recognition, or via aesthetics. The User and the Hunter both relate to power, but the Hunter usually already has a sense of power and is looking to maintain it, while the User probably has no power and is searching for a partner for the sole purpose of trying to get power or status.

The User is looking for their partner to solve problems in their lives that they haven't personally been able to figure out, such as financial literacy, emotional security, or a sense of power over their own lives. This sets up a perfect environment for a toxic dynamic to develop because the User is placing responsibility on the other partner to maintain their own personal stability *and* to compensate for their own lack of skills and lack of development.

## Exercise: Identify Toxic Types in Your Past

After reviewing this section, take a few moments to reflect on past relationships in terms of these types.

- Did any of your past relationships fit into these discussed vignettes? Put a check for your partner and/or for you. Remember, both parties can fall into these categories; it's not always all or nothing.

| Type | Your Partner | You |
|------|------|------|
| The Distressed | | |
| The Catch | | |
| The Hunter | | |
| The User | | |

- What behaviors did you or your partner exhibit that match any of these types?

# THE PILLARS OF A TOXIC RELATIONSHIP

For a toxic relationship to develop between two people, seven conditions or behaviors tend to be present: trauma, the habit of tolerating harmful behavior, confusion, an all-or-nothing mentality, manipulation, deception, and inauthenticity. These conditions and behaviors are often modeled in the foundations discussed in Chapter 1—areas like family, friends, media, and so on—while the person was forming their ideas of what a "healthy" relationship looks like. In this section, you'll explore these pillars of toxicity.

Within the following discussion about pillars of a toxic relationship, you will see a few key terms. The *precipitator* is the person prompting the issue. The *tolerator* is the person enduring the issue. The *sphere of influence* refers to parent, sibling, peer, friend, religion, and media influences that impact your perception of what is normal and/or healthy in a relationship. Each pillar outlines what both the precipitator's and the tolerator's internal narratives may sound like to help you get an idea of how these issues form and are rationalized by the people involved.

## PILLAR 1: TRAUMA

This involves observing relationship trauma in your sphere of influence. It creates a sense of normalcy around harm and is where the idea that pain and trauma are normal comes from.

- **Precipitator Thinks:** *Pain is normal, so if I am causing pain for others, that is to be expected. If they are saying it's my fault, it's because they aren't strong enough.*
- **Tolerator Thinks:** *Pain is normal, so if I am in constant pain that is to be expected. If they continue to make choices that cause me pain, that is to be expected as well because that is how "normal" relationships operate.*

## PILLAR 2: TOLERATING HARMFUL BEHAVIOR

This involves watching your sphere of influence continually tolerate harmful behavior. By continually tolerating harm and then presenting that harm as real love, it is building to a toxic understanding of relationships.

- **Precipitator Thinks:** *If they think what I'm doing is harmful, that is their issue.*
- **Tolerator Thinks:** *I tried to tell them they were harming me but every time I attempted to hold them accountable, I ended up feeling responsible for the whole fight. Eventually, I wouldn't bring up any issue anymore because it was not worth the fight. This is just how things are, so I have to learn to live with it.*

## PILLAR 3: CONFUSION

This involves watching your sphere of influence be consistently confused or embedded in chaos or unpredictable dynamics and then seeing them peddle this off as typical.

- **Precipitator Thinks:** *My partner says that they are confused but if they were actually invested in our relationship, they would just know what I'm thinking.*
- **Tolerator Thinks:** *I am super confused all the time. I attempt to read my partner's mind but their mind seems to change day to day and I feel like I can't do anything right. I guess I am the problem.*

## PILLAR 4: ALL-OR-NOTHING MENTALITY

This involves watching your sphere of influence say things like, "You either love me or you hate me" or "You either support me or you don't" in their relationships. The all-or-nothing mentality doesn't allow for the mix of emotions that occurs in every relationship. For example, you can love someone *and* hold them accountable for the way they are hurting you.

- **Precipitator Thinks:** *Either they are in this relationship or they are out. Regardless of my behaviors, if they continue to stay, that's on them; I'm not forcing anyone to stay.*
- **Tolerator Thinks:** *Any doubts I have make me feel guilty, because I can't be both in love with my partner and angry and confused and upset; I have to choose one emotion.*

## PILLAR 5: MANIPULATION

This involves watching your sphere of influence manipulate their partners into behaving a certain way. They may weaponize sex, money, the home/security, the children/custody, therapy, or any type of self-growth.

- **Precipitator Thinks:** *Sometimes I have to manipulate my friends and family because they just don't see my side of the story. My half-truths aren't really hurting anyone; they just don't get that relationships are complicated. If I told them everything, they wouldn't understand.*
- **Tolerator Thinks:** *Sometimes I feel like I'm going crazy. I see signs that our relationship is unhealthy but when I ask my family and*

*friends about it, they tell me that my partner is "doing their best" and that they are a good person and I just need to hang in there. I feel so isolated because it feels like I'm the only one who sees the problem.*

## PILLAR 6: DECEPTION

This involves watching your sphere of influence continuously lie to get what they want, teaching you that if you want something or someone, lies may be necessary to make it happen.

- **Precipitator Thinks:** *If I have to lie sometimes in my relationship to keep the peace, so be it. That's how every couple I know avoids fights.*
- **Tolerator Thinks:** *I know they are lying but I think they lied to protect me from more pain and I can understand why someone would do that.*

## PILLAR 7: INAUTHENTICITY

This involves watching your sphere of influence create fake personas, get defensive when someone calls out their inauthentic tactics, or teach you how to fake your emotions to keep others happy.

- **Precipitator Thinks:** *If people knew how I actually acted no one would really like me, so I have to put on a good face for my friends and family and colleagues. People rarely see my true self.*
- **Tolerator Thinks:** *My partner is a completely different person when we leave the house but I do my best to also put on a good face and make sure people aren't aware of the tumultuous environment we actually live in.*

## WHEN TOXICITY BECOMES YOUR NORM

When a person witnesses any of these pillars consistently enough, or is directly involved in them enough, slowly but surely the mind develops an understanding of what is "normal" or "acceptable" in a relationship based on those unhealthy behaviors and conditions. The person then brings these understandings to their intimate relationships, modeling what was shown to them. It is a cycle of toxicity, with each person taught harmful ideas about relationships growing up to then repeat and teach those ideas to others in their lives—who go on to do the same.

Once expectations are set about relationships, it's difficult for both precipitators and tolerators to recognize the unhealthiness of the dynamic. When someone attempts to tell a tolerator, for example, "Wait, what they are doing to you is harmful" or "That situation sounds incredibly unhealthy," many times the tolerator will get upset and defensive. They might claim things like, "You are just jealous because you don't have someone" or "Your expectations for people are too high." When someone attempts to say to a precipitator, "Do you talk to them like that all the time?" or "You need to respect them; that is messed up," the precipitator will also get upset and defensive. They might respond, "Mind your own business; this works for us, okay?!" In essence, they'll do anything to remain in that "this is normal" mentality.

If toxicity has been normed, then anyone pointing out that something is toxic feels like a threat. The psyche struggles to make sense of that dissonance (the disconnect between what you know deep down and what you have normalized), and then the person draws conclusions that the pain they are enduring must make sense because if it doesn't make sense that might mean they are in a harmful relationship—and that is a difficult thought for most people to admit. If the precipitator gets called out, it's not in their best interest to admit the implications of their behavior because to admit that would mean they must be held accountable for their behavior. A precipitator will never break the cycle of harm if they never gain perspective that their harmful behaviors truly disrupt the people around them, especially the people they claim to love.

The primary work of learning how to heal from a toxic relationship will be in self-reflection and processing the pain that has come from the unhealthy foundations modeled for you during early development.

*The primary work of learning how to heal from a toxic relationship will be in self-reflection and processing the pain that has come from the unhealthy foundations modeled for you during early development.*

## TOXIC RELATIONSHIPS ARE BUILT ON A LACK OF INTERNAL VALUE

Looking through the pillars of toxicity, you can see a pattern: A toxic relationship starts when one partner is going into the relationship with a mentality that the relationship will heal parts of themselves that have never been addressed. The Distressed partner wants to be rescued, the Catch needs admiration, the Hunter needs to maintain power, and the User wants to gain power.

All of these needs stem from the partner not knowing their inherent value and instead attributing their value outside of themselves. The problem is that because they only see themselves as valuable in relation to others, they aren't able to be alone because alone they are worthless. They think they only have value or power when someone is telling them they have value or power.

This basic dynamic of looking for external validation is in direct conflict with the definition of a healthy relationship. If a person thinks (whether consciously or not), *I need to be in a relationship to feel valuable*, they are operating with a misunderstanding of the purpose of a relationship. A relationship doesn't define your value; a relationship honors your value. The value is already there. Many people don't establish a firm sense of their own value before dating and then they jump from relationship to relationship on a never-ending quest for their purpose, power, or value—which is inside them all along. They are looking for someone to confirm that they are lovable, rich enough, attractive enough, or smart enough, but it's impossible for another person to do that. That has to come from inside. You are not someone else's purpose; you are their partner. You did not create their value. You are not the origin of their value, and they are not the origin of yours.

## Internal versus External Value

Let's say an artist creates a piece of art. When finished, the artist stands back and marvels over their beautiful creation. The art is valuable to the artist. Along comes Jade, an art enthusiast. The artist shares their art with Jade and Jade agrees that the artwork is truly stunning. The question now is, What made the art valuable? The creator of the art or the appreciator of the art—or a blend of the two? What if the artist only saw their art as valid, beautiful, or worthy if other people defined their art as such? What if they created art depending on what was popular that day? What if the only value they felt was fleeting because it wasn't anchored to their own perceptions of their inherent talent but to the whims of pop culture? It would seem odd for the artist to operate like this, instead of assessing the value of their work on their own. Yet this is how many people go through life—only seeing their value through others.

When you establish a sense of value within yourself, you start entering relationships with a new mindset. You are not looking to form a relationship to create your value. You are entering a relationship to honor the value you bring. If your partner didn't see themselves as valuable and only looked to the external for that value, they started the relationship asking for something from you that you could not give them: an identity.

## COMMON BEHAVIORS IN TOXIC RELATIONSHIPS

If a partner doesn't have a firm sense of their identity or their own value, they will often adopt certain behaviors in order to secure a sense of control and power over the relationship. These toxic behavior patterns are maintained through methods related to power, control, and confusion.

You may recognize some or all of these patterns—either from the beginning of your time together or as the relationship deepened. You'll need to heal from each of these patterns, so it's important to be aware of which ones you were exposed to. Love-bombing, passive-aggressive tactics, neglect, gaslighting, testing loyalty, blame-shifting, and buffers are all elements that help identify if a toxic relationship is brewing. If you have seen these methods and watched your partner justify themselves and their actions or lack of actions for engaging in these methods, that is a solid sign that a harmful pattern has developed. Let's learn more about each one.

## LOVE-BOMBING

According to a study called "Love-Bombing: A Narcissistic Approach to Relationship Formation," love-bombing is the act of trying to exert power and control over another person's life through excessive displays of love early on in a relationship. Love-bombing might look like showering a person with emotional and physical gifts at the start of the relationship, so as to manipulate them more easily down the road.

- Examples of **physical gifts** include jewelry, clothes, flowers, and, in some cases, larger-ticket items, like surprise trips, offering to pay rent, or buying you a new car.
- Examples of **emotional gifts** include adoring text messages; showing up to your workplace just to say "I miss you"; spending time with you; telling you repeatedly how much they love you, how beautiful you are, or how lucky they are that you chose them. It might also look like playful "fantasy" statements, things like, "I can't wait to marry you" or "I can't wait to start a family with you."

You might be thinking, *Wait, that is how* all *my relationships felt in the beginning, even the good ones*, and you're right, there is some nuance here. Being in the infatuation stage of a relationship may have you vibing in that "new relationship energy," but that is very different than love-bombing. The clear indicator of toxicity is that with love-bombing, the person showering you with gifts is doing so to create a false sense of established reality for the relationship. Not only is love-bombing incredibly harmful; it has a distinct feature that is not occurring after the infatuation stage: devaluation.

When your partner starts the relationship with love-bombing, it feels amazing. It's nice to be showered with gifts, vacations, emotionally rich conversations, and cute texts. It can feel like a dream to have a partner who seems attuned to your needs and emotionally available. The issue is when things change and you no longer feel those things—in other words, you are devalued. Devaluation is a behavioral and emotional shift that occurs in a relationship when a partner who was previously elevated, cherished, and adored is now either insidiously or dramatically depreciated or debased. The shift is not always obvious in the moment, but it is usually clear when reflected upon after some time has passed.

### THE PROBLEM WITH LOVE-BOMBING

Love-bombing serves several purposes for partners with toxic tendencies:

- **It establishes a deep connection very fast.** The relationship moves forward very quickly, which allows the partner who is searching for connection and stabilization to feel comforted and relieved when they think they are quickly bonding with a new partner. In relationships with love-bombing, that connection is a lie.
- **It creates a false sense of continued love and adoration.** When they come on so strong at first, the natural logic is to assume that your new partner will continue, even in small ways, to show affection like they did in the beginning of your relationship.
- **It creates a false identity.** A false identity in a toxic relationship is when the toxic partner crafts an identity that is an idealized version of themselves. It's a manufactured persona, typically crafted in the weeks leading up to the relationship, or the first few weeks or months in the relationship. The false identity serves them well when they start the devaluation phase, because they can point out to anyone questioning them that they are an amazing partner because they bought trips and gifts and food for their partner. They justify their actions by pointing out that although they treated their partner badly, that was just a fluke,

and they will soon be going back to treating their partner like a gift. With a false identity, the partner can believe that their good partner will be back at any time. The partner tolerating the debasement might hold out hope that their "old partner" will come back. If things continue to be terrible, they might threaten to leave the relationship, which is the cue for the partner who is love-bombing to start the cycle over. This looks like starting to send gifts again, or writing notes saying things like, "You are my everything" or "Don't give up on us!" Thus starts another cycle of idealization and devaluation.

## PASSIVE AGGRESSION

Passive-aggressive communication is a way to say something without *really* saying it. This behavior pattern is utilized in toxic relationships when a partner does not have the skills to communicate their actual needs or intentions. For example, if someone was looking for their partner to save them financially, but they did not want to be blatantly honest (to themselves or others) about that, they might make comments like, "Well, my last girlfriend helped me pay for my car insurance because she was generous." The person doesn't want to admit that they want someone else to pay their car insurance, *and* they want their partner to feel guilty by implying that they are not generous if they don't.

### THE PROBLEM WITH PASSIVE AGGRESSION

The passive-aggressive partner won't address their lack of relationship skills or personal autonomy skills. They will instead try to convince you that it is *your* responsibility to provide them with whatever relational skills they are lacking. The truth is, both partners are responsible for cultivating interpersonal skills and they must work together to practice those dynamics inside of the relationship. The more passive-aggressive one partner is, the more the other will actively avoid difficult conversations for the sake of maintaining some sense of stability.

## Case Study:
## The Pitfalls of Passive-Aggressive Communication

Brad (who uses he/him pronouns) fits into the Distressed partner category (see Types of Toxic Partners earlier in this chapter). The method he implements while starting to navigate issues in the relationship is passive aggression. Sky (who uses they/them pronouns) is attracted to Brad because Brad is sweet and funny, but he also has a lot of issues that Sky immediately feels an urge to help with. Brad tells Sky that his car is in the shop and that he loves partners who are super considerate and giving. Brad immediately starts to assume that Sky will loan him their car whenever they aren't using it.

At one point, Brad takes Sky's keys while they are at work, and when Sky asks Brad about it, Brad (utilizing passive aggression) says, "I don't know why you are upset—you weren't using it." Sky says that they would have been fine letting Brad use the car, but they are more upset that Brad didn't ask first. Brad shrugs off Sky's concern, showing a lack of respect for basic communication, and Sky starts questioning if they are overreacting.

While this example seems like a small misunderstanding, consider this dynamic going on for years. If you tap into the thematic depth of this issue you can see that Brad is struggling with communication skills and Sky is showing up with a basic level of communication skills. Brad then rejects the communication request, does not listen to the actual problem, and passive-aggressively redirects the conversation to the issue being with Sky's reaction to the lack of communication. Sky walks away confused and wondering if their request was "too much."

## NEGLECT

Neglect is a relational method where one partner withholds engagement, love, time, effort, or their presence to get what they want. This method doesn't allow time for processing emotions; it is a weapon. Strategically disengaging without emotional processing is a toxic trait.

## THE PROBLEM WITH NEGLECT

Neglect is a tool for manipulation and punishment. The partner who is refusing to address their emotional needs is only perpetuating that problem by using neglect as a shield to "protect" them from having to face that challenge of processing. Partners who are suffering from neglect can begin to experience low self-esteem and symptoms of depression and/or anxiety. A partner who neglects you and your request for authentic connection, communication, and processing is telling you that they may not:

- Have the emotional navigation skills to process that issue.
- See that your needs are as important as theirs.
- Care enough to work on the relationship.

In a relationship, neglect can look like:

- A partner withholding praise if you accomplished something great.
- A partner refusing to listen to your concerns about the health of the relationship.
- A partner withholding any physical engagement that was previously established (for example, if you typically cuddled while watching a show but now your partner sits on the other side of the couch and refuses to acknowledge the change in physical connection).
- A partner consistently forgetting birthdays, anniversaries, or important events that matter a lot to you.

## SILENT TREATMENT

The silent treatment is a severe form of neglect that's very common in toxic relationships. Giving the silent treatment is not just having a brief break during a tough conversation; it is a deliberate disengagement for days or maybe weeks. Many people who engage in this relationship tactic were modeled this when they were younger. They may have even been subjected to this exact method by their parents, teachers, or friends. The neglect during silent treatment looks like complete disengagement. For example:

- Your partner refusing to acknowledge you are in a room.
- Your partner turning the lights off on you when they leave a room.
- Your partner walking right past you and refusing to respond to any type of conversation that you initiate.
- Your partner speaking to "nobody" to communicate a request; this looks like: "Boy, I wish Sara was here to do these dishes."
- If you don't live together, it might look like complete blackout on digital communication—no texts, calls, DMs, or responses—when you are attempting to converse about the disagreement you had.

This tactic is emotionally abusive because, on top of shutting down the processing of any real information about why the fight happened, it's incredibly manipulative. Typically, the person enduring the silent treatment begs the partner who is disengaging to "come back," or they apologize for communicating a relationship issue, saying something like, "I'm sorry I brought it up; please just let's go back to normal, okay?"

This becomes a cyclical behavior because the partner perpetuating silent treatment doesn't seek healing or new information; it is just a waiting game until the other person forgets or gives up.

## Constant Confusion

When two people start a new relationship, it's normal for them to have little misunderstandings as they get to know each other, but *constant* confusion is not a sign of a healthy beginning. If one partner is constantly confused, it's important to find out why. Some common reasons for confusion to be constantly present include a lack of communication, authenticity, or honesty, or the presence of gaslighting, blame-shifting, or deflection.

Constant confusion is a sign of a harmful relationship dynamic. Constant confusion is not normal; it is harmful. It is usually a sign of a partner who is not showing up to the relationship in a real way and not being honest with themselves about how they are acting in the relationship.

## GASLIGHTING

Gaslighting is the term used when a person manipulates someone into questioning their own sanity. The partner with toxic tendencies may say things like, "I never said that," "That never happened," or "You're remembering that wrong," which leads the other partner to ask themselves, *I know what I saw; am I going crazy?*

When someone consistently creates a situation in which they deny the other person validation or verification that a scenario played out in a certain way, a person can start questioning their own reasoning or viewpoint when recalling a memory or a trauma. Gaslighting is a trauma in and of itself, because when a person's reality is slowly shifting around their partner's perceptions, they no longer feel as though they can trust their own conclusions of events and the partner then is free to craft scenarios into anything they want them to be.

### Case Study: Gaslighting Is a No-Win Situation

Shawn constantly criticizes his girlfriend Liz for not wearing better clothes, saying they are boring and not visually appealing. Because of the comments, Liz goes out and buys a few sundresses, comes home, and puts one of them on. Shawn's immediate response is, "Why are you wearing that? What do you want, attention or something?" Liz starts to think she is going crazy because just yesterday Shawn told her that she needed better clothes and now today Shawn acts as if wearing the better clothes is absurd.

The recurrent behavior here is Shawn is making comments and then getting angry when Liz attempts to change her behavior. This is where you get the "Damned if I do, damned if I don't" feeling that many people in toxic relationships can relate to. In a situation where gaslighting is consistently occurring, you really can't win—and you might even leave the situation questioning your own perceptions and your own processing of basic situations.

## TESTING LOYALTY

Another toxic behavior is using loyalty tests to create a dynamic in which one person has complete control. A harmful partner wants someone to "Jump when I say jump," so they will create opportunities to "test" the loyalty of their partner. Many people who endure this kind of mental abuse start to lose sight of their own preferences. They stop thinking about if *they* are happy and begin to focus on just keeping their partner happy. By constantly having to prove themselves, they begin a pattern of no longer considering their own wants, desires, and needs.

For example, let's say Shawn plans a date night on the day of Liz's family reunion. Shawn is testing to see if Liz will choose him or her family of origin, whom she cares for dearly. Shawn is setting Liz up to fail and testing out Liz's loyalty to him. He is seeing just how much Liz will bend to his expectations.

## BLAME-SHIFTING

Blame-shifting is a form of deflection. It is when a partner is asked to hold themselves accountable for an issue or a problem, but they shift the conversation drastically into an offshoot of the original issue. Blame-shifting is very concerning since it's a clear indicator that the person you are dating or married to does not have emotional navigation skills.

Blame-shifting is a simple defense mechanism that is often present in children but also found in adults who haven't learned relational skills. Blame-shifting is sometimes also called *whataboutism*, which is referencing the tactic involved when a person brings up an issue such as, "I need us to talk about how much money you are spending," and then the partner responds with, "What about you? Like you've never bought too much online!"

Blame-shifting is a sign of emotional immaturity. The partner is unable to hold space for any emotion other than their own. They see your frustration as a threat to recognition of their own emotional frustration. A person who is emotionally mature and emotionally skilled knows that two frustrations can coexist; they don't have to compete with each other.

---

### Case Study: Deflecting Is Avoiding

After an evening out with friends, Tom says, "Kim, I was really upset when you made fun of me in front of my friends at dinner." Kim responds, "Like you've never said anything bad about any-one else your entire life, Tom? Get over it!" Kim did not address Tom's original issue; she instead redirected the energy back onto Tom. Tom might immediately start to defend himself and get wrapped up in the deflection, saying something like, "Kim, give me one example of when I threw you under the bus in front of my friends." With this response, Tom is entertaining Kim's redirection and they both are now discussing a different issue instead of processing the original point.

It's important to note that if Kim truly wants to discuss with Tom how he engages in the same behavior, that is valid and justi-fied. But when it's only brought up as a way of deflecting, it's less productive. In conversations like these, the goal should not be to unload every problem you ever had with the other person. It's best to remained focused on the one issue that is being present-ed. If more issues arise, honor them another time.

---

## BUFFERS

A buffer can be anything that deflects you and your partner from processing the real issues that are going on in the core of your relationship—like the physical or emotional gifts related to love-bombing mentioned earlier. The biggest problem is that buffers are surface-level solutions to deep-rooted problems. When some couples fight, one partner buys chocolates, flowers, a little gift, or their partner's favorite snack the next day. While this is cute, if this behavior occurs after a particularly difficult argument, it can be a red flag. Take a step back and think about what might be happening with these gifts. Is the gift simply being used to communicate love—or is it being used as a buffer? For the purposes of this book, think of a buffer as something that bypasses (or "buffs" away) the true event that needs to be processed.

Let's say two partners get into a fight and one partner calls the other a whore and then throws a laptop across the room. If the laptop thrower later brings chocolates and says, "I'm sorry," the chocolate can become a buffer. Without the chocolate, the next conversation they have is more likely to proceed toward asking the pertinent question: How do we have conversations together without the threat of violence? But with the chocolate, the partner could be attempting to bypass that conversation and buff out the tension in hopes that they have evaded true accountability for their actions. The emotionally unskilled partner may even bring up the chocolate if the other attempts to go to the thematic depth of the issue. They could say, "Why are you making me feel bad about it? It's over! I get you chocolate and you do this to me!?"

The toxic trait here is using chocolate to manipulate. True accountability occurs when the laptop-throwing partner acknowledges the implications of their behavior, recognizes the harm caused by that behavior, and participates in a discussion to identify skills, strategies, and tools to assist in learning a new way of engaging in the relationship. In no way is chocolate enough.

---

### Non-Gift Buffers

Buffers don't have to be physical gifts. They can also look like your partner buying you lunch the next day or planning an impromptu trip in hopes of distracting you from the fight. Unplanned buffers exist, too—for example, a medical event, like a child getting sick right after you have a fight with your spouse. Because both of you are focusing on getting the child to feel better, it feels cruel to bring up the fight from a few days ago.

---

Relationships where buffers are used frequently often start to feel circular—a difficult moment happens, a buffer helps smooth it over without really addressing the underlying issue, then another issue happens and the cycle continues. With each cycle the relationship feels worse and worse, because no real solution or progress is happening. All that is occurring are small little tokens of remorse without real conversation around creating the skills it takes to elicit change. It is brief awareness without committed action for change.

## Exercise: Name Buffers You Have Experienced

Use these prompts to help you identify elements in your past relationships that were buffers.

- Try to think of a memory or an event that didn't get resolved because of something else that soothed away the stress or distracted you from the processing.
- What were some specific things that were used to evade real processing? (List gifts, events, holidays, obligations, etc.)
- How did buffers contribute to the lack of depth in your relationship with your partner?
- Think about a time when you attempted to get to the root of the issue:
  - How did your partner respond?
  - What solutions were proposed?
  - Who proposed those solutions?
  - Were those solutions executed and followed through on?
- What themes can you draw from this exercise?
- What skills do you want to develop based on the themes you identified from this exercise?

## LOOKING BACKWARD, THEN FORWARD

This chapter has outlined many key components of toxic partnerships. It's important to be able to analyze what happened previously, then use that knowledge in a positive way going forward. If all you do is identify issues but brush off the underlying dynamics that it took to sustain that toxic relationship, the cycle will not end.

Starting now, your reflective mind is your true power. Skills and strategies are your biggest strengths. You are no longer just going with the flow. You are becoming anchored, with knowledge, awareness, and ultimately skills to establish a deep foundation within yourself. This strong sense of self will help you break the toxic relationship cycle.

## Exercise: Recognize Thoughts versus Actions

In this chapter, we've discussed many techniques and elements found in the toxic relationship dynamic. By understanding how your partner acts and your response to that partner, you can analyze and address the deep underlying issues that cause these toxic methods. Once you understand those things, it's vital to engage in action beyond thought. Thoughts are not enough to achieve complete healing. Acknowledging that a dynamic had many toxic elements is important, but taking action will help you move forward to healing and future healthy relationships.

For this exercise, we're going to examine some deep thoughts you have about a toxic relationship and how each thought turned into an action. Here's an example:

*What relational aspect of my partner did I find attractive?* [the thought]

I love giving and supporting. I am attracted to people who I can immediately help and be of service to. I find that I see myself as a valuable partner in so much as I can add value to their life by being everything to them.

*How did that attraction influence the way I show up to relationships?* [the action]

I show up to relationships wanting to be wanted. While that is a valid need, it creates a high likelihood of someone taking advantage of my giving heart. I give and give and my past relationships would take and take and then I would be angry and resentful and miserable.

Now you try. Ask yourself:

- *What relational aspect of my partner did I find attractive?* [the thought]
- *How did that attraction influence the way I showed up to the relationship?* [the action]

Now that you have this information, you can begin to shift away from any habits that don't serve you. You're going to ask yourself: *What skill would be useful for me to gain in the future that will assist me in ending this cycle?* To follow the example, we could say: "I need to develop a healthy level of giving and support to my partner while simultaneously not forgetting about my own needs."

A shifted mindset then looks like:

- I want to give to my partner and my own needs are important.
- I want to support my partner and I deserve a partner who is equally supportive.
- I want to be available to my partner and I am allowed to have time to myself and time to nourish my own individual friendships and visions for my life.

## KEY TAKEAWAYS

- Relationships that start with harmful expectations create toxic foundations.
- Manipulation can be intentional or unintentional.
- Unintentional manipulation is common among partners who have little to no emotional processing skills.
- The observation of "the precipitator" and "the tolerator" during your development played an important role in how you conceptualize relationships and repeat toxic patterns.

- Blame-shifting and buffers are used frequently in relationships that struggle with emotional processing and emotional communication.
- Breaking the toxic cycle involves identifying and practicing new skills and creating new perceptions about yourself.

# CHAPTER 3

# HOW TOXIC RELATIONSHIPS NORMALIZE TRAUMA

"I don't know who discovered water but I'm pretty sure it wasn't a fish."
—Anonymous

Just like fish, we don't know that we are steeped in certain environments until we are taken out of them. If your past relationship created an environment that was very unhealthy, but it was sold to you as typical, normal, and a standard practice for relational interaction, then questioning it would be unreasonable. You might have never questioned your relationship until it was unraveling. Many people don't see the issues until well after the fact. The further you are from being embedded in a toxic dynamic, the better you can see the problems that occurred. We can't heal from what we don't know is there.

Don't judge yourself harshly if you missed any of the signs in Chapter 2—many people don't fully notice or understand the issues while they are fully involved in them. If your past relationship was very unhealthy, but your partner behaved as if everything was very normal, then you may not have questioned any of it. The further you are from being embedded in a toxic dynamic, the better you can see the issues that occurred. This perspective is important because in order to heal from trauma you have to know the wounds are there.

In this chapter, we'll examine the process by which the toxic behaviors you learned about in Chapter 2 become an accepted part of a relationship. Understanding more about how a toxic partner controls the relationship will help you unravel the effects of the toxic relationship and begin to heal from it.

## NORMALIZED TRAUMA IS UNTREATED TRAUMA

Just because something is labeled as normal doesn't necessarily mean it is. While some may contest that there is no such thing as a "normal" childhood, what is important to note is there *are* harmful behaviors and harmful beliefs that get perpetuated throughout generations. When those are played off as acceptable and typical, the trauma that is sustained because of those behaviors and beliefs now gets overlooked, underevaluated, and checked off as a typical Tuesday in your home. Likewise, because trauma associated with toxic relationships is often slowly introduced and gradually integrated into your relationship, it can be very difficult to identify.

Think back to Chapter 1, when we discussed the norms associated with your earliest relationships—those with your immediate family. Children rarely question their living environments. If your mother used to wake you up every night because she was cleaning the house at 2 a.m., you probably assumed every mother did that. If your father used to ignore you for days on end and never hugged you, you probably assumed that's typical of any father. Likewise, imagine a couple who swears at each other during a fight. If that habit started early on in the relationship and one partner never said, "Absolutely not; do not talk to me like that when we are in a conflict," the partners begin to normalize that behavior. No matter what your particular norms are, eventually they will show up in your intimate partnerships.

When you have been separated from the toxic dynamic for a few months or a year, you might see the narrative change. That's when you start to think, *Wow, how did I not see how harmful that was at the time?* Unlearning harmful norms is essential for healing and recovery.

## WHAT IS COMPLEX TRAUMA?

According to Judith Herman in the book *Trauma and Recovery: The Aftermath of Violence—From Domestic Abuse to Political Terror*, complex trauma is prolonged, repeated trauma. Complex trauma causes harmful disruptions in a person's identity formation and sense of self. This is trauma that becomes integrated into a person's everyday life. It occurs in dynamics where a person perceives they don't have the ability to practice autonomy because their environment indoctrinated them into believing they have no power or control over the situation. Many times in these situations, from the outside looking in, it looks like the person has full autonomy to leave these dynamics. But in reality, people with complex trauma are typically in deeply bonded relationships with their family, faith, friend groups, workplaces, or partner. The intricate value system built around these bonds makes it very difficult to leave the situation because it might feel like their only known source of "love" or connection. I sometimes use the term *insidious trauma* when explaining complex trauma because it helps people understand the true nature of this kind of trauma. Complex trauma is slow and creeping and you may not realize it has occurred until someone points out just how problematic it is.

I developed the acronym DRIP to help remember the particular nature of complex trauma:

- **Duration:** The trauma is endured for a long period of time.
- **Repetitive:** The trauma happens again and again.
- **Insidious:** The trauma proceeds in a gradual or subtle way.
- **Persistent:** The trauma continues to exist despite attempts to mitigate it.

The DRIP acronym also evokes the added visual of the trauma slowly dripping over you. A small drop of trauma seems like nothing, but when those drops keep coming, you eventually realize you are about to drown.

Complex trauma is especially tricky to identify because most individuals who experience it may not recall a single specific event that the trauma is linked to. Instead, they recall a pattern of interactions that occurred with their loved one over a long period of time. For example, a wife constantly belittling her husband, a boyfriend constantly mocking his partner because of their weight, or a partner who gives the silent treatment every time a conflict occurs. If you took the individual incidences of, say, "They called me a cow" or "They didn't talk to me for a few days," some people might excuse that as, "Oh, they were just having a bad day." But if you take those incidences and add them up over weeks, months, and years, that is what complex trauma is. It is built brick by brick; but because it happens so slowly, you might not be able to notice how much pain it is causing you even though it's staring you in the face.

## COMPLEX TRAUMA IS A SPECTRUM

Complex trauma exists on a spectrum. Typically what you see referenced as complex trauma are the most extreme examples, such as being raised in a cult, experiencing human trafficking, or being a prisoner of war. What is often missed is when complex trauma integrates into society so well people don't see it at all. Here are a few examples of complex trauma that are worth noting:

- Bullying/cyberbullying
- Violence/physical abuse
- Consistent threats of violence
- Emotional abuse
- Marital/partner rape
- Being exploited as a child (child labor, being parentified, being weaponized in a custody battle)
- Emotional neglect
- Physical neglect
- Being a victim of grooming/love-bombing
- Financial abuse (weaponizing money to gain control over you)

- Spiritual abuse (weaponizing the idea of God to gain control over you)
- Workplace abuse (your workplace using their position of power to exploit your time, energy, or mental health)

With complex trauma existing on a spectrum, it's tempting to think we can organize these traumas in a hierarchy, but that is not the right approach. The traumas listed here and all the variations of the traumas found deep within those categories are not in competition with each other. *There is no trauma hierarchy.* Even if you didn't endure the most extreme examples of complex trauma, your pain is valid and your trauma is allowed to be called trauma. Whether a person has endured abhorrent ongoing trauma or very subtle and covert trauma, both traumatic experiences had implications on the person's life. Both people are allowed to heal. You can drown in two feet of water or you can drown in the ocean—but no matter how or where it happens, anyone drowning in trauma deserves healing.

*There is no trauma hierarchy.*

## WHEN COMPLEX TRAUMA IS COVERT

Covert trauma is trauma that is difficult to see at face value. While complex trauma can be very obvious to some, when it is covert it is difficult to see, both for the person experiencing it and for anyone on the outside looking in. It is called covert because, depending on the context, many people dismiss the experience as "typical conflict" or "having a hard day." It's the epitome of "normalized trauma."

Let's review some types of behaviors that are often found in unhealthy relationships and can lead to covert complex trauma:

- **Ongoing criticism:** Constant criticism, degradation, nitpicking, microaggressions, shaming, and blame-shifting.

- **Ongoing neglect:** Silent treatment, dismissal of core needs, being told your existence is inconvenient.
- **Ongoing parentification:** As discussed in Chapter 1, parentification occurs when a child must assume a parent's or adult's responsibilities, such as:
    - Being an emotional support system for the parents.
    - Taking care of a parent when they are dealing with substance use.
    - Acting like an adult friend if parents disclose information such as sexual experiences to their children.
    - Disclosing or dealing with financial hardships that the child truly does not understand due to their developmental age.
- **Ongoing enmeshment:** An enmeshed family (as we discussed in Chapter 1) is a perfect example of complex/insidious trauma because most families that have this dynamic have no clue other families exist with personal boundaries and autonomy. It seems so normal to them that to question the family's expectations would seem absurd to them. Intimate partner enmeshment can look a bit different than family enmeshment, and Chapter 5 will go into much more detail about what that looks like.

## Exercise: Identify Traumatic Patterns

Take a moment to identify elements in your past relationships that were potentially traumatic. Think of your past intimate relationship(s), then answer the following questions:

- Where did most of the conflict come from?
- What topics were frequently tension points?
- How did your partner perceive alone time or private conversations?
- Did you feel like your partner "owned" you?
- Note a time where you tried to express yourself and that expression was weaponized against you (for example: "I need space" turned into "Oh so you are going to abandon me now?!").

- How was self-improvement or mental health talked about in the relationship?
- How was self-advocacy viewed?

Read through your answers and come up with three patterns or themes you can identify within your responses. Keeping those themes in mind, complete the following sentence as many times as you need. Listing these traumatic behaviors will help you accept what happened in the past, and also acknowledge that these behaviors are not acceptable in future relationships.

When I was with them, I thought _____ was normal yet _____ is not normal.

When I was with them, I thought _____ was normal yet _____ is not normal.

When I was with them, I thought _____ was normal yet _____ is not normal.

Finally, reflect on what you want to change going forward. For example, you might say: "I need to find a partner who respects healthy amounts of privacy so I can tend to my own needs."

- What skills would you want to develop from the themes you identified from this exercise?

## KEY TAKEAWAYS

- Complex trauma is trauma that happens slowly over a long period of time.
- People in relationships that have normalized harmful dynamics struggle to identify core issues that need to be addressed within the relationship.
- The DRIP acronym and dripping visual can be useful for understanding what complex trauma can look like in your life.
- Covert trauma is trauma that is difficult to see at face value.

# CHAPTER 4

# KEEPING UP THE CHARADE

In toxic relationships, looks can be deceiving. When you are in a relationship that is controlling, harmful, or emotionally immature, a split emerges: You have (1) the relationship that other people perceive you are in and (2) the actual relationship that you are in. The perception that others have of you in the relationship becomes almost like a script you follow—a part you play. The outside world sees a happy version of you, while the reality can be anything but.

In order to keep the peace, you may be "playing your part" to act like the happy couple because you don't yet have the tools to remove yourself from the relationship. In this chapter, you will learn more about how and why you end up pretending things are okay in a harmful relationship, the different ways this charade can present itself, and how to begin shifting from the pretend to the authentic.

## WHY YOU CREATE A CHARADE

When you are in a relationship, it can be very difficult to acknowledge the amount of toxicity you are enduring. As explored in Chapter 3, this toxic behavior becomes normalized, so many people find it hard to accept the truth, especially in the early stages of healing. Additionally, there are a lot of complex emotions, difficult questions, and uncomfortable thoughts behind harmful relationships. Although the problems in the relationship may not be reasonable, some people play pretend because it seems easier than facing those tough emotions and thoughts, and because it feels too painful or even embarrassing to let other people see the reality of what they are going through.

You might find yourself posting to social media cute pictures of you and your partner with the hashtag #couplesgoals or #happilyeverafter so no one—including you—dares to question the reality of the situation. If you tend to people-please, being a part of the charade may be an external manifestation of your people-pleasing tendency. You want the people you love, including those who may harm you, to be happy, and as a result you may choose playing pretend over potentially upsetting anyone.

## FAKING IT

Faking happiness becomes the norm for those who learn that if they call out their partner's behavior, they will be met with volatile emotional and/or physical reactions. For these people, faking it feels safe in an environment that does not accept the truth of the relationship. It is the only way you may get any semblance of peace while in the relationship. Things that are commonly faked in toxic dynamics are:

### Sexual Interactions
- Faking pleasure.
- Faking orgasms.
- Faking whether or not you are in the mood.
- Faking whether or not you are willing to try certain sexual acts.

### Emotional Interactions
- Pretending you are okay.
- Avoiding difficult emotional conversations.
- Faking happiness/contentment.
- Pretending you are not upset.

### Physical Interactions
- Hugging your partner when you don't want to.
- Cuddling your partner when you want to be alone.

- Kissing your partner even when you are angry with them.
- Holding your partner's hand in public so people don't ask questions.

### Spiritual Interactions
- Pretending you are religious when you are not.
- Pretending you have the same beliefs about faith as your partner.
- Pretending you are on the same page spiritually as your partner when you aren't.
- Pretending to be happy at church when you are miserable.

If your partner has become emotionally or physically abusive when you have tried to have an honest conversation about your needs or desires in any of these areas, you may have felt it was safer to just fake it so your partner wouldn't demean or demoralize you.

---

### Case Study: A Sexual Charade

Jen and Adam started dating about a month ago. They have been having frequent sex. Recently, Jen has been struggling with reaching climax during penetration. She starts a conversation about adding a vibrator as well as asking Adam to attempt to stimulate her in other ways to help with climax. Adam immediately gets defensive and says, "What, my body isn't good enough for you?" Jen is shocked by his response and jumps to soothe his ego: "No, no, I love having sex with you. I am bringing this up because I am not reaching climax anymore when we are intimate." Adam then replies, "Well, I'm not going to compete with a vibrator and all my other girlfriends never complained."

Recognize how Adam did not actually take the time to hear what Jen was communicating to him. Jen simply wanted to learn how to have a better sex life with her partner. Adam took any conversation about sex as an insult instead of an opportunity to grow together. Jen replies, "Okay, I'm sorry," apologizing for being authentic, open, and honest with her partner, then adds, "just forget I said anything." Jen has learned that she is going to have to fake orgasms with Adam in order for him to not get upset with her.

When you are scared to be honest and authentic with your partner, there is a reason. Something has happened within your dynamic that is perpetuating a charade. Sometimes it's the partner's response to your attempt to be authentic, and sometimes it's your own fear from past relationship traumas. Many people may struggle to not project a previous partner's toxic response onto their new partner, regardless of how healthy the new relationship may be. The new partner then gets confused because they haven't acted unreasonably or reactively.

So how do you know where your urge to fake it is coming from? When you find yourself scared to be real with your partner, ask yourself this: Has your current partner shown signs of reactivity to your authenticity?

If the answer is no, it is likely that past relational trauma has steered you toward hiding your authenticity in this new relationship. If this is the case, talk about your past relational trauma with your current partner. Explain how you are attempting to practice showing up authentically and challenging the fear that is lingering from your past relationship(s). This communication will be helpful in clearing up your partner's confusion and encouraging you to heal from the trauma still impacting you.

> *When you find yourself scared to be real with your partner, ask yourself this: Has your current partner shown signs of reactivity to your authenticity?*

If the answer is yes, you are scared because there is clear evidence that your current partner does not allow a safe environment for you to safely express yourself, then validate that. Tell yourself, "This is not in my head; this is real. I feel unsafe. I feel as though I can't be real with my partner. I feel trapped because every time I am open, I get punished." Validate, validate, and continue validating. That validation will build self-trust over time; it will build conviction and belief behind your experiences and a new foundation for self-advocacy.

## Exercise: Reflect On Your Experience with Faking It

Take a moment and think about a time in a relationship that you felt like you had to fake it. Recall all of the areas (sexual, spiritual, etc.) where people fake it, and think about what aspect felt the most painful to suppress. With this in mind, use a journal or blank piece of paper to follow these steps:

1. Write about a time in your relationships when you found yourself faking your true feelings. Write down as many details as you can remember surrounding this situation. (For example, times you told a friend "everything's fine" when it wasn't, or times you pretended to be happy when you were not happy at all.)
2. Write about the particular elements you felt weren't safe to explore or articulate to your partner. (For example, times your partner made you upset, and may have even asked you, "What's your problem today?!" and you responded, "I'm fine.")
3. Write about a time when you tried to show up with your real feelings about something that was upsetting you.
4. Write about your partner's reaction when you attempted to show up with your truth.
5. Write about what happened as a result of your partner's reaction to you showing up with your truth. What pattern(s) did you fall into regarding being authentic going forward? Did you begin avoiding discussing a certain topic you knew would make them reactive?
6. Write what you wanted to say in that situation when you were faking it.

## THE PAIN BEHIND THE CHARADE

Why is playing pretend in a harmful relationship so painful? Why is that pain even there?

Pain is a communicator. While no one typically seeks out pain, pain being present inside of your body or your mind is there to tell you something important. It is your job to decipher it—uncovering where it came from and what it is communicating to you.

Let's say a gymnast rolls their ankle during a practice move. Despite being in pain afterward, they don't tell anyone out of fear of how the coach could react, or how their teammates might perceive them. The pain is telling them to rest their ankle, or even get it checked out by a professional for bigger issues—yet the gymnast might choose to ignore this and pretend everything is fine on the floor. When asked about how they are feeling, they might blatantly lie and say they feel great when they are really in immense pain. As they continue to ignore it, the pain grows. When you play pretend in a harmful relationship, you are that gymnast walking around and practicing on an injured ankle. Because you have ignored the pain, you become more injured over time, as you are having to pretend that an injury isn't there. Whether a gymnast hiding a rolled ankle or a partner faking happiness, playing pretend is lonely, isolating, and miserable. It only builds more pain over time.

## WHEN THE PAIN GETS OUT

That emotional pain that you hide when you play pretend in front of others or fake it with your partner has to go somewhere. It can't just evaporate—as much as you might wish it would. After a while, it will find its way to the surface.

Repressed pain will often either release itself inward (showing up as self-hate) or get projected onto other relationships (like your relationships with your children, friends, or coworkers). Because you feel safer expressing yourself internally and with people who do not berate you or punish you for your authenticity, these are the relationships that will get the brunt of your pain. You might get super angry at a friend for a small mistake, feel resentful toward yourself for not knowing something, or be hypercritical of a coworker. This can create strain or hurt feelings in those other relationships. And while emotional processing may happen in these situations, it is not happening with your partner (which is actually the only place that pain processing would elicit real change). That disconnect is how people can spend years in toxic relationships that remain unchanged.

## APPROACHING THE PAIN WITH COMPASSION

As you begin healing from a toxic relationship, it's critical to develop compassion for the person inside of you who created the charade. Why is this important? Because that past version of yourself was trying to protect you. They were trying to keep you safe and avoid very painful moments for you. The beautiful part of all this is that now you are in a period of growth and self-awareness. As you move through this book, you are approaching the pain, the dissonance, and the difficult realities of your toxic relationship, and taking important steps toward healing. Give yourself the grace and patience you deserve along the way.

## THE END OF THE CHARADE

When you are ready to drop the mask and realize that the source of your pain is not yourself or a friend or coworker, but your relationship, you can start rediscovering your authenticity—and recovering from your toxic relationship. Of course, this journey will come with its ups and downs. Because you endured so much and are now left picking up the pieces, you may be feeling vulnerable. You may want to immediately replace your old charade with a new one. Or you may want to fill in that gap of your past relationship with new relationships, new religions, new friends, or new interests.

While new things can be incredibly healing and helpful toward your recovery, they are not a substitute for learning new relational skills. It is these skills that will help prevent toxic situations in the future. It is likely that at some point, someone else will speak over your power, attempt to silence your truth, or belittle your dreams. Healthy relational skills will be your guide in not giving this person any consideration—let alone any agency in your life.

Although you will be working more in depth on these skills in the second half of this book, here is one strategy for you to start practicing right now: Follow the resistance. Pay close attention to internal tension such as resistance or dissonance. This tension points to key opportunities for growth. When you find yourself struggling to open up on a date with a new love interest, follow that resistance. Let it lead you to a new skill that your mind is begging you to learn. Get comfortable with looking at the things in your psyche that create tension—and what they are telling you.

## THEIR REACTION

When you decide that you are done playing pretend and your partner realizes this, they may resort to gaslighting. It can sound like: "What are you talking about?," "I never said that," "I never reacted that way," "You were always allowed to tell me anything." The person doing the gaslighting is refusing to acknowledge their part in a toxic situation. They are refusing to hold themselves accountable for the harm they have caused. (Partners may have reactions other than gaslighting as well—we'll cover this more in Chapter 5.)

If your partner refused to acknowledge how they hurt you or played a role in creating a toxic relationship, you may be left doubting yourself, questioning your reality, and underestimating your pain. You have spent a significant amount of time being told your needs aren't important, are inconvenient, or that you overthink everything. Once the charade has ended and you have begun recovering from the relationship, you may start to question if your standards are too high, or whether your partner was really "that bad." You may question if you were making up all of these issues in your head (*Maybe I'm going crazy?*) and should just "let it go" and take the partner back. You may be the hopeful romantic type who creates a fake version of your partner in your head and hopes that they might one day fit that image and begin treating you the way you deserve to be treated. Facing the reality is essential to combating your self-doubt here. Looking at the relationship for what it has been, not what it *could* be, is not only a practice in your own radical self-honesty, but a big step forward in healing.

> ## Case Study: Letting Go of the Charade
>
> Rae was in a relationship with her partner for three years. She is in the early stages of recovery from that relationship. After it was clear that the relationship was ending, she was left feeling worthless, ugly, and angry. She was upset that she wasted three years with someone who treated her so poorly. She started to realize the primary emotions she was feeling were anger and resentment. She resented herself for not noticing how bad it was and for playing the perfect girlfriend for families and friends.
>
> During the relationship, when her friends would voice concerns, she panicked because she knew that the charade was slipping. Eventually, she realized that this panic was linked to the fear that she had to come to terms with just how damaging the relationship was. That fear wasn't the enemy; it was an informer. The radical truth was that Rae was scared to be alone, and she was scared that all the bad things her partner said about her might be true.
>
> Rae's situation is all too common. By learning how to let go of the charade, Rae can start to process the true nature of her experience of the relationship with authenticity, and tapping into that authenticity is a fundamental part of recovery.

## WHY DID IT TAKE SO LONG?

When looking at their toxic relationship with a new, honest lens, many people may think, *Why didn't I see it sooner?* or *Why did it take me so long to get here?* The truth is that sometimes the psyche simply isn't ready. Sometimes when you are going through a tumultuous relationship, you aren't emotionally able to process the truth just yet. Processing that truth is difficult. It is perfectly valid that your journey took longer than expected. The important part is you are here today, reading this, and well on your way to recovery.

Just like when thinking about how you came to create the charade, it's so important to practice self-compassion for the previous version of yourself who wasn't ready to tackle the truth. Maybe you weren't ready then, but you are ready now; take a moment to appreciate what that means. You have grown, you have developed new thought patterns, and you have allowed your mind to process painful experiences. Shaming your past self for not having the information that you have now only creates self-hatred. It's time to focus on valuing yourself—on rebuilding the authenticity and confidence that was lost during the relationship. You are valuable, you are important, and you are worthy of real love: Say this now, and return to it as needed along the path to healing.

## KEY TAKEAWAYS

- Pretending that you are happy in your relationship can be prompted by difficulty in accepting the truth, avoiding uncomfortable or painful conversations with others, or fears of reactions from your partner.
- Emotional safety being threatened encourages and strengthens a pattern of faking it.
- The emotional pain you are hiding has to go somewhere; if there is nowhere safe to put the pain it either gets suppressed or released in unhelpful ways.
- It takes time to create enough distance from a harmful dynamic to be able to gain the perspective that change must occur. Have compassion for yourself and celebrate where you are now.

# CHAPTER 5

# CODEPENDENCY AND THE TOXIC DYNAMIC

Enmeshment and codependency are two unhealthy ways that people can exist in a relationship, and they're both often found in toxic relationships. Enmeshment (which we touched on briefly in Chapter 1) refers to having blurred boundaries between the self and the relationship—a partnership where at least one person is not allowed any privacy. Codependency is where one partner bases their self-worth around their partner's life and makes their decisions stemming from that perception. It is a mature version of enmeshment that incorporates the sense of self as the hallmark feature.

In codependent relationships, your perception is that you are not allowed to be an individual, and because of that your self-esteem can suffer. You can also find yourself taking too much responsibility for the other person's behaviors or choices. Instead of focusing on what you want for your life and how that can integrate well into a partnership, you're focused on what's best for your partner and only your partner. You become an afterthought; your needs become inconvenient to consider because they will typically get in the way of your partner's needs and, when codependency is at its worst, you considering yourself is categorized as selfish and egotistical. In this chapter, you'll learn more about enmeshment and codependency and their effects both on you as an individual and on the relationship itself.

# ENMESHMENT IN PARTNERSHIPS

In intimate partnerships, enmeshment looks a lot like control and a lack of individualization. This behavior might form because of family history, such as if a family didn't allow anyone to be an individual. If people don't unlearn family enmeshment before they start dating, they are likely to continue that pattern and have the same demanding expectations of their romantic partner. Enmeshment occurs when two individuals are not allowed to have personal boundaries. Because they are not allowed to have individual boundaries, the two parties psychologically blend into a collective. Because they have blended together, their decisions become entangled and the partners start to struggle with making decisions for themselves. In enmeshed partnerships, you don't know where one person ends and the other begins.

Enmeshment is a hard concept to grasp; because of that, it's important to provide you with examples. While reading through the examples, you may see similarities between your partner's expectations, your family of origin's expectations, or both.

An individual in an enmeshed couple struggles with making decisions without discussing every aspect of that decision with their partner. This is not to be confused with a couple who likes to be considerate of each other's needs. A person who is enmeshed convinces themselves they are just being considerate, kind, or thoughtful when what is actually happening is they are losing their own place of priority in their own life.

Think of the couple who is unable to see themselves as individuals and *only* views themselves as a collective. This means they no longer get to make individual decisions and they no longer get to have individual opinions or an individual outlook on life; everything is a collective. An enmeshed couple will look at individualization as selfishness. They were not taught how to consider themselves in the equation and therefore must consider their partner before all other things, including their own desires or needs.

By noticing how enmeshment shows up in relationships, you can be equipped with the tools needed to unlearn what passed for normalcy in your past toxic relationships. It is painful to realize past relationship patterns that you precipitated or tolerated were brimming with harmful behaviors, yet the only way you learn how to get past some of these defaults is by first identifying that they are there and then actively seeking new skills to strengthen you for the future.

## Codependency versus Enmeshment

Enmeshment and codependency are close cousins. *Enmeshment* describes behaviors and actions under the codependency umbrella. Enmeshment is more about blurred boundaries in interpersonal interactions and the entanglement that happens in a particular relationship or relationship system (like a family/church group/workplace). Remember, a hallmark of enmeshment is that everyone knows everything about everyone and no one is allowed privacy or individuality. *Codependency*, on the other hand, is more about the value and worth gained from being needed and feeling overly responsible for another person's function. People who tend to find themselves in a codependent dynamic typically struggle with breaking up, because when they realize the relationship is no longer functioning, they fear that by ending the relationship they will no longer feel needed—or worse, they will feel responsible for the other person's downfall.

Enmeshment in personal relationships can take the form of harmful accountability, harmful reliance, or harmful disclosure; you'll learn about each of these next. Keep in mind that some of the following categories have quite a bit of nuance, so it is a good idea to read this section more than once, especially if anything you read starts to cause tension for you. Don't let the tension worry you; it could indicate an area of potential growth for you. We will more thoroughly cover how to deal with tension in Part 2 of the book. For now, simply notice any tension around these topics with a curious mind, and start practicing accepting that tension without judgment.

## HARMFUL ACCOUNTABILITY

*Isn't accountability a good thing?*, you may be asking yourself. Yes, for the most part. Accountability becomes harmful when it refers to needing to report to your partner where you are at all times—in other words, a lack of personal autonomy and relational trust. These are relationships where one person demands passwords, GPS coordinates, and check-in texts in order to keep very close tabs on the partner. Harmful accountability is one way enmeshment can show up in your life.

Needing a partner to be always accounted for is a sign that one person does not have a baseline trust of the other. Their trust may have been broken by some past event in the relationship, or their capacity for trust may be lacking due to past relationships or childhood norms.

*Needing a partner to be always accounted for is a sign that one person does not have a baseline trust of the other.*

### Genuine Concern about Safety versus Enmeshment

Of course, not *all* requests for your location indicate enmeshment. For example, if you're staying in a hostel in another country and your partner asks you to check in to ensure you got in safely, you can see the good intentions behind that request. But that request should be communicated as such so the concern is clear. If a person circumvents that communication skill and jumps right into, "You must share your location with me," their partner may get upset and feel like they have a parent-like figure hovering around what they do, and they might resent their lack of freedom.

### BUILD TRUST, NOT TOXIC ACCOUNTABILITY

Establishing trust in a relationship should include honoring your own needs while listening to your partner and respecting the relationship that you are a part of. Let's say you want to go to a place that might be concerning to your partner—a strip club, for example. In a healthy relationship, you'd start by acknowledging that you'd like to go somewhere that your partner might not appreciate you going. Then, you have a choice: You can either have a conversation with your partner and discuss mutually agreeable parameters around you going, or you can lie and say you won't go… but then actually go. If your partner wouldn't want you at that location and you go anyway, you are hiding part of your true expression of self, and you have shown that you don't have the skill to navigate a hard conversation.

Is it concerning that you went to a place that your partner would not appreciate? Sure. Yet, what's perhaps even more concerning is the fact that instead of having an honest conversation about the strip club, both parties may not have the relationship skills to navigate a difficult conversation like that without it being a blowout fight. If the partners don't have the ability to manage difficult conversations, the relationship will develop norms that bypass that skill development. These norms can look like GPS apps, text check-ins, and a slow decrease in autonomy to make up for the lack of skills. If both self-trust and trust in your partner are established through externals (texts, GPS, passwords) and not cultivated deep within the self or the relationship, the relationship is founded on a lack of authenticity and trust.

## Is It Convenience or Control?

Important note: This is a nuanced topic. Some couples say that sometimes digital disclosure is useful, such as sharing a password with a partner. In cases such as these, assess the thematic depth of the issue. Are you disclosing your passwords for convenience or for control? If this is out of sheer convenience, like your partner logging into an account to send a message for you, the rationale is not control. It takes radical self-honesty to come to terms with what kind of dynamic is occurring in a relationship. If the sharing of the password is founded on a lack of trust that your partner won't be faithful, that is helpful information to process. No password or GPS app will truly ever give you a grounded sense of trust. Trust is built and cultivated internally and stems from immense self-work.

## HARMFUL RELIANCE

Much like accountability, reliance isn't always a bad thing. Relying on your partner to be there for you in difficult times is perfectly natural. Relying on them for things that should have been nurtured within yourself is a whole other story—that's harmful reliance. It is a subset of enmeshment and is an example of how enmeshment can show up in your life.

Let's explore this with an example of self-care and exercise. Let's say your partner wants to start exercising more. They make a commitment to themselves to take a walk every day. They may start by asking you, "I want to go on a walk every day. Will you go on the walk with me?" This eagerness for better health is their vision and their goal and you agree to walk to be supportive. This seems harmless, at first glance. Let's say you walk together for a couple of days straight, and then you have a work meeting one day and can't walk.

What happens next? In this example:

- **Harmful reliance** would look like your partner deciding they won't walk because you aren't going with them. They may later say, "Well, I *would* have gone on a walk, but you weren't available." They are putting the responsibility of their personal self-care back onto you.
- **Healthy autonomy** would look like your partner walking without you because they see themselves as an individual and can achieve their goals on their own.

Healing from harmful reliance and enmeshment means you are able to stand up for your individual needs, hold yourself accountable, be radically self-honest, and rely on yourself. It also looks like not saying sorry to your partner when they made a conscious decision to not take a walk that day, because their decision to walk every day is not your responsibility. This is not to say that a partner's support isn't valuable—it is—but support is not the same as responsibility.

## HARMFUL DISCLOSURE

Emotional expression is very important in relationships; but when that disclosure starts to harm yourself or others, we move into the "harmful" category. Harmful disclosure is the act of oversharing information with your partner, to the point of losing your sense of privacy in the relationship.

Have you ever met someone who says, "I tell my partner everything"? At first glance, this looks innocent and could be a sign of deep intimacy. But for many people, it's a sign of difficulty with personal boundaries and enmeshment. For someone who never learned boundaries around self-disclosure, it feels second nature to share every thought, every emotion, and every issue. It's important to understand when disclosure is honoring the self and in alignment with processing—and when disclosure is stemming from a place of feeling as though you need to justify, report back, or validate every thought, emotion, or belief.

### PRIVACY VERSUS SECRECY

When a child is trying to learn where their family ends and they begin, it's easy for the child to think that any thought that they don't share with their family is a "secret." For some, they avoid feeling like they're hiding something by disclosing every thought, emotion, and issue they have.

In an enmeshed family or relationship, privacy or internal processing of emotions or events is viewed as secretive or bad. To a toxic partner, privacy is a threat; it means you must be hiding something. Yet the two are very different:

- **Secrecy** is not disclosing information that is necessary for both parties in the relationship to be aware of.
- **Privacy** is a healthy way to honor internal and external boundaries and allows for individual development.

When a relationship has no trust, no sense of boundaries, and no room for individual processing, any type of private individual work is deemed unacceptable. The toxic partner will weaponize that separation and tell their partner that they must want to break up, they have to be cheating, and they aren't loyal if they don't share every single thing with them. Sadly, this possessiveness over their partner many times stems from past relationship traumas.

### Case Study: Tracking People's Movements Will Backfire

Jill has experienced a lot of relationship trauma. Her past partners all cheated on her and she has always blamed herself for not being "enough." She also has slowly stopped trusting people, including her new partner, Dan. Because of this trauma, she perceives that any time Dan is quiet it must mean that he is keeping something from her. She perceives that any time Dan comes home late it must mean that he is cheating on her. She perceives that any time she has good sex with Dan it must mean that he learned that new trick with another partner.

Because Jill is so paranoid, Dan does his best to have clear communication with Jill, but he starts getting upset that Jill demands justification for everything and she accuses him of not being "open enough." Dan feels violated because he doesn't think it's fair to have to report every location, every extra minute to his partner. He feels like he has no personally owned time and gets resentful toward Jill. Dan gets angry because he never did anything wrong in the relationship, yet Jill treats him like he is not worthy of her trust. Jill senses that resentment, which fuels her suspicion even more. Although Dan hasn't ever been unfaithful, he is finding himself wishing he was out of this relationship because he feels like he has no autonomy, and that Jill is suffocating him. Jill's attempts to track and control Dan are actually backfiring—instead of bringing her closeness and comfort, they're only pushing Dan away.

# HOW PARTNERS PERPETUATE TRAUMA IN A TOXIC RELATIONSHIP

In a relationship where toxic dynamics are normalized, the toxic partner may need to use several different techniques to keep the relationship going. Partners who do not have emotional skills will make every effort to maintain a sense of normalcy surrounding their poor behaviors. They'll tout their demanding expectations as reasonable or claim their lack of engagement within the relationship is acceptable. Let's discuss a few ways partners may attempt to keep toxic dynamics normal.

### WATER UNDER THE BRIDGE

Have you ever tried to discuss a difficult topic with your partner and your partner said, "Why are you bringing *this* up? That was two days ago; get over it!" The problem with that is that a couple needs a healthy opportunity to process situations that caused pain. How will anyone ever learn what skills they need to gain if no one wants to talk about an event, discussion, or situation that did not go well?

Some partners need a bit more time to process a fight that recently happened; that's fine. But a partner who refuses to reflect at all on an issue that caused disruption to your relationship is telling you, "I do not tolerate someone holding me accountable for the way I show up to situations." If your partner is not willing to be held accountable, then there is no way a relationship can grow.

### SETTING A PRECEDENT

A precedent is an act or instance that serves as an example or justification for subsequent situations. Partners who struggle with accountability will use a past precedent to justify their current behaviors. Not all precedents are bad, but depending on how precedents are set, they can be an important factor in maintaining a toxic dynamic.

For example, if a person is used to having their partner's passwords to all their accounts, they could in theory tell their partner, "I did this with everyone else and so I expect to do it with you as well!" They did not analyze whether sharing every password is healthy and did not consider their partner's thoughts on the matter.

Setting precedents in relationships that are based on past unhealthy relationships is bringing the old into the new. If you want to recover from the past, it's essential to reflect on why these precedents were set in the first place. You may have set precedents from past relationships, you may have endured them, or you may have experienced a blend of both. Either way, part of the normalization of toxic dynamics can be found within certain precedents from the past. The goal is to set new healthy precedents and bring in those new expectations to create growth within yourself and your new relationships.

## A GRUDGE OR ACCOUNTABILITY?

Holding a grudge and holding someone accountable are two different relational strategies.

- A **grudge** is harboring ill will or resentment toward someone. The person has not processed the emotions around the situation. Instead, at times they weaponize that information and present it back to the other person in order to create more harm.
- **Holding someone accountable** is bringing up past issues to serve a purpose or function for growth or skill development. Your aim is not to harm the other person by processing past pain; your aim is to process the experience together, so you can grow into a stronger couple and learn from that past pain.

If your partner can't tell the difference between a grudge and accountability, any type of conversation about a past experience could be misunderstood as holding a grudge.

## Case Study: Navigating a Difficult Conversation about Accountability

Tim and Diane occasionally disagree about finances. Tim makes less money than Diane and Diane tends to be a little more unrestrained with her spending habits. Tim notices that Diane never likes to talk about their spending habits. Tim calmly attempts to discuss a few late bills with Diane, now that they have blended their finances together. Tim says, "Diane, I'd like to talk a bit about our bills." Diane immediately freezes and says, "Ugh, not this again." She is very dismissive toward Dan, a sign that she may not be able to emotionally navigate this conversation. Tim says, "Diane, I know this is a hard conversation, but it is important. Your spending is something we need to talk about—it is starting to affect our ability to pay our mortgage and bills. I am helping out as much as I can, but we need to discuss our financial stability."

Because Diane does not want to admit she has an issue with her spending, she uses emotionally immature skills to go on the offense. She deflects and says, "Like you don't have any issues, Tim!" Tim replies, "I do have issues, and if you want to talk about some things that upset you that I do, we can. But let's tackle one issue at a time and stay on topic so we can have a productive conversation." Now, Tim brings up a specific situation from the past to help Diane understand the magnitude of the issue with her spending and its effect on everyone. Tim says, "Diane, last year when you went on that spending spree, I had to cover the mortgage payment with my entire paycheck. Because of that surprise expense, I didn't have enough money to buy my nieces and nephew Christmas presents. That really affected me, so we need to figure this out together."

Diane now perceives this moment as a grudge, which it is not. Tim is not attempting to bring up this issue to harm Diane; he is bringing up the past situation in an attempt to shine light on how Diane's spending affects multiple people. Diane says, "So are you going to hold that over me for the rest of my life?!" Tim replies, "No, Diane, I don't bring any of this up to hurt you. I am attempting to process past situations that caused relationship strain so we can learn through these issues together. I want us to figure this out together." Tim is simply requesting that Diane listen and attempt to problem-solve, which shows that Tim really cares about Diane and wants to figure out a way to solve this. When a partner is emotionally unskilled, as Diane is, however, grudges and accountability feel the same.

## A DEEP DIVE INTO CODEPENDENCY

*Codependency* is a buzzword in the psych community, but it's often not fully understood. Codependency is a relational pattern where one partner has a strong value system around feeling needed and develops their sense of self-worth around their partner's life. This means that one partner defines a need and the other partner anchors their worth as a person around tending to that partner's need. This becomes problematic quickly in dynamics where one person is harmful and demanding and the other person is getting fulfilled by meeting the demands of their partner. The relationship becomes unbalanced almost immediately and by default one partner is not being personally responsible for their own needs and the other partner is becoming entrenched in the needs of the other person (and typically neglecting themselves and their own needs).

A healthy partnership is a mutually shared agreement in which both partners are freely giving their love and fully showing up to their lives, fulfilling their individual responsibilities. A toxic relationship is a relationship where the dynamic is off-balance. Expectations are skewed, perceptions are warped, and love is weaponized. This person being depended on is not limited to a romantic partner; the "other" can be a best friend, parents, siblings, or children. The purpose of exploring codependency in this book is to explore perceptions around love and belonging. When you better understand these perceptions, you can start to challenge old narratives and develop new ones.

## CODEPENDENT...OR JUST CONSIDERATE?

How do you know if a person is just being considerate of their partner or if the relationship is codependent? The answer is in the details, the intentions, and the feelings behind a behavior. In short, a codependent partner struggles with their individualization, while a self-sovereign and considerate partner will be able to consider their partner's needs alongside their own. They'll use their emotional navigation skills to articulate and balance those coexisting needs. Here are some other key differences to consider:

### Person in a Codependent Partnership

- Feels trapped in the relationship and will struggle to make decisions without their partner's input.
- Struggles with their own identity.
- Might base their identity on traits of the other partner. For example: Your partner likes sports and suddenly you must be into sports now as well (even if you don't like sports).
- Feels like they aren't able to operate as an individual.
- Feels guilty for wanting to do things for themselves (like being alone, having their own interests or hobbies, or having individual friendships).

### Person in a Considerate and Self-Sovereign Partnership

- Feels the freedom to make individual decisions.
- Understands their individual identity.
- Looks at themselves as both an individual and a partner.
- Feels the freedom to make time for themselves and their aspirations or desires while remaining attentive to their partner's needs.
- Takes time to explore their individual interests.
- Does not force their partner to be something they are not.
- Respects the differences in their partner and does not see those differences as a threat.
- Looks at their partner as an individual who is also in a relationship and respects their own space as well.

# BEHAVIOR PATTERNS COMMON WITH CODEPENDENCY AND A TOXIC PARTNER

When we break down the particular patterns seen behaviorally in codependent relationships, certain themes arise. Understanding what fuels codependent traits and identifying the fear and motivators that are involved in these traits can help pinpoint areas for growth in recovery.

## YOU ARE NOT ALLOWED TO BE AN INDIVIDUAL

Codependent relationships can occur when enmeshed behaviors seep into the relationship expectations. A classic example is if your partner is drinking too much and they start to expect you to drive them to their AA meetings to keep them sober. Because you aren't always available to take them to every meeting, your partner blames you for their lack of sobriety because you aren't prioritizing their sobriety. In reality, however, you are just trying to have their needs and your needs coexist. Because your partner doesn't see a boundary between their problems and your problems, their problems *become* your problems. If you don't take on their problems as your own, you are deemed selfish. You are told, "You don't even care about me." They are telling you, "You are not allowed to be an individual," without saying that out loud. Any time you feel trapped or in a place where your needs feel like they are in competition with theirs, start to get curious about codependency. It's important to note the difference between a considerate partner and a codependent partner in this example:

- A **considerate/self-sovereign partner** will do their best to support their partner's sobriety and at the same time continue to hold their personal boundaries strong. So, they might be helpful on one or two occasions where their partner might need a ride, and they will also be letting their partner know that they will not be available to be their *only* source of transportation for their meetings.
- A **codependent person** may try to set the same boundary, but feel guilt and shame if they have an important obligation that

conflicts with giving their partner a ride. A codependent person will always choose their partner first and ignore their individual needs. So, if the codependent partner had a doctor's appointment during the AA meeting, they would cancel it and prioritize their partner's health over their own. Seeing a boundary in this situation would sound like: "Hey, I am not available next week. I will need you to arrange another ride for your meeting." But because a codependent person absorbs their partner's issues, problems, and concerns *as their own*, asking their partner to find another ride makes them feel like a selfish partner, and in order to avoid feeling like a bad partner, they neglect themselves.

Another way codependency shows up is when one partner becomes entrenched and overly invested in their partner's life. Let's say one partner is trying to find a job. A codependent partner would immediately look at that problem and start taking that problem on as their own. They may spend hours searching for the perfect job for their partner. They might print out job postings or even apply to jobs on behalf of their partner. On the outside looking in, this can look sweet and profoundly supportive, but by taking on the responsibility of finding a job for them, the codependent partner is not allowing them to develop their own much-needed life skills, like job searching. This behavior then creates the "over-responsible/under-responsible cycle."

## Codependency and Boundary Issues

The toxic partner has no regard for boundaries because boundaries are an impediment to accessing and manipulating another person. A codependent person has little to no boundaries because they are scared if they have them, their loved one won't love them after they enforce the boundary, or the partner will abandon them if they enforce the boundary. This creates a perfect storm for toxic dynamics.

## OVER-RESPONSIBLE/UNDER-RESPONSIBLE CYCLE

In this cycle, one partner is overly responsible for things and the other partner is under-responsible. This mechanism is found in codependent relational systems. The partner who is being under-responsible can range from innocent ("Sure, you can search for jobs for me, if that's what makes you happy, babe") to incredibly toxic ("If you loved me, you would find a job for me"). The more harmful partner will weaponize that distorted view of "love" and continue to reiterate that you are a terrible partner if you aren't taking responsibility for their life and their obligations.

In this cycle, the partner who is being over-responsible truly believes that they are being a good partner and the partner who is taking advantage (the under-responsible one) might believe that it's reasonable for their partner to take on those responsibilities. This may function in the short term, but in this cycle, one partner is being neglected completely while the other partner is being centered in the relationship and everything now revolves around them and their contentment. This breeds misery, resentment, and burnout for the over-responsible partner.

## Case Study: Over-Responsible Behavior in Action

Brit has an anxious attachment style but doesn't realize she has codependent tendencies. She just started a new relationship with Jake and she is head over heels for him. Brit grew up in a home that was very dysfunctional and she felt as though she had to earn her family's love during her childhood. Jake immediately picks up that Brit needs constant reassurance in her relationships. He realizes that she adapts to whatever he says. He also realizes that she sees all of his problems as her problems and uses that as a weapon.

Jake had a big test coming up that he was studying for. Brit was being very supportive and helping him make flash cards and staying up late to help him study. The night before the test, she fell asleep while helping Jake study. Jake stayed up a bit longer to study those last few cards before the test. Jake took the test and failed. He came home and told Brit that the reason he failed was because she was too lazy to help him study. Brit realizes he is talking about when she fell asleep, and she starts apologizing to him and telling him that she will help him every day until the re-test. Jake not only did not take responsibility for his test results; he convinced his partner that she was the main reason for the results.

Brit doesn't agree that she was the main reason he failed—but she doesn't feel safe to articulate that. She is scared that if she approached Jake with the reality that his test is ultimately his responsibility that Jake would break up with her. Instead, Brit defaults to taking on the fault because the alternative in her mind is losing Jake.

## PERCEPTIONS SKEWED: EXTERNAL VERSUS INTERNAL FOCUS

People who struggle with codependency have an external focus on life. They tend to disregard themselves and they may even neglect their own voice completely. Because of that, the external reigns supreme and dictates that person's happiness. The external focus can be on anything: grades, salary, and/or another person's approval or praise.

The person with codependency is therefore off-balance because their psyche is meant to balance both external and internal. When someone experiences their value only from the external, it can become very dangerous, very fast. It is dangerous because the external is constantly changing and unpredictable. And if the external is constantly changing, so is your value. That emotional roller-coaster ride can be very difficult to manage. Additionally, if a person develops their value only from an external narrative, their internal narrative weakens. People with codependency will feel happy if they can make other people happy and ignore it if they are upset internally. The internal voice that says, "Hey, you are valuable regardless of what that person next to you is saying," might even eventually go unheard because it has spent years being neglected.

Think about how this dynamic could play out in relationships. Some people think a relationship is *for them* and that's it. It's not based on mutual consent and autonomous giving. The relationship is all about *how it serves them*. So, if a vulnerable person whose value is based on the external ends up with this type of toxic partner, that toxic partner has all the control. They are vulnerable because if the person with codependent traits couples up with a harmful partner who is manipulative and coercive, the toxic partner will then dictate that person's existence and identity.

## HAVING TO PROVE LOVE ISN'T REAL LOVE

If you were raised in a family that told you the only way you can receive love is by doing something for it, there is a high likelihood you may have codependent tendencies. It's not always family that forms this issue; it can also result from past formative relationships if you were told (consciously or subconsciously) that the only way you can receive love is by proving there is something in it for the other person. If this habit sounds familiar, love becomes dependent on what you do, not who you authentically are.

If you've been in relationships like this, you learn that the only way you can feel loved is by fulfilling other people's needs so you can prove your love for them and then in turn they can love you back.

# Case Study:
## Recognizing Authentic Love and Boundaries

Mal and Tina have been dating for a few months. Mal is really into football; Tina isn't. Mal invites Tina to go to a game with her and Mal made sure she told her it was okay if she didn't want to come. Tina doesn't trust that Mal is actually okay with her not going. Tina remembers a situation from her last relationship—she and her ex had a disagreement and her ex told her, "It's okay, Tina, just go to sleep." Tina wasn't sure what the right thing to do was but she did go to sleep. The next morning, her ex-girlfriend was visibly distraught and made a comment about how she was "left alone" last night and that Tina must not care about the relationship at all.

Because of situations like this with her past relationships, Tina doesn't trust people's authentic answers. She constantly reads between the lines, even if there is nothing to see. Tina forces herself to go to the football game even though she doesn't want to be there because she thinks, *That's what good girlfriends do.* She feared that if she didn't go to the game, Mal would secretly be mad at her, so in order to show Mal that she is a good girlfriend, she ignores her true feelings about football and forces herself to go anyway. Tina is now resentful and angry that she keeps having to go to things she doesn't want to despite Mal consistently saying, "Tina, I don't want you to ever force these kinds of things. You are allowed to not like the same things I do." This creates a huge tension point in their relationship because Tina is resentful and Mal is confused. Tina felt as though she could not be an individual in her relationship with Mal, even though Mal reiterated multiple times she could be. Tina was struggling to trust that she was safe to be an individual because of her experience with a past toxic relationship.

## A LOSS OF SELF-ESTEEM

People who are in a codependent relationship with a toxic partner will report that they feel like they are never enough. Because to "be enough" in a toxic relationship would be impossible; the toxic partner always wants more. The toxic partner learns quickly that your self-worth is dependent on what they say to you that day. They know that your self-esteem is a roller coaster because they know how much power they have when they tell you things like, "You look gross in that," "No one cares about your opinion," or "Stop talking; no one cares." They know you rarely, if ever, consider yourself first. They know that you don't have the counter voice that speaks up and asks the question, "Okay, I know my partner said that no one cares, but let me ask myself, do I think that is actually true?"

When a person's value is dependent on their partner's feedback, in a toxic relationship that feedback can be weaponized to get you to do things, be things, and believe things that aren't aligned with your true self. Your authenticity gets thwarted—and in some cases altogether decimated.

## ANXIOUS ATTACHMENT AND CODEPENDENCY

People with an anxious attachment style will constantly seek reassurance about the relationship. These are the people who "check in" all the time about the relationship. They ask, "Hey, are you mad at me?" or "Do you still love me?" after a conflict. This attachment can stem from childhood and often gets affirmed in early intimate relationships. Anxiously attached people can easily find themselves exhibiting codependent tendencies, because in order to feel that reassurance they are seeking, they try to engage in behaviors that meet that yearning to feel important or needed. They also spend a lot of time avoiding the possibility of abandonment. They might clean their partner's car or buy their partner lunch out of fear that if they don't do those things, their partner will abandon them.

In a toxic relationship, a harmful partner will latch onto and perpetuate the narrative that you aren't enough. They might even bring up past relationships that they abandoned due to their partner not meeting their every need. Because now there is proof that your partner will abandon you if you aren't constantly showing outward signs that you care about them, you will panic if you aren't constantly checking in or pouring out your love to them in various ways. A toxic partner will confirm to you that your greatest fear will occur if you don't jump when they say jump or act the way they want you to.

### INTENTION IS EVERYTHING

Let's say you'd like to buy your partner lunch. A good practice is to take a moment and consider your intention for doing that. Are you allowed to buy lunch for your partner? Of course! But there is a huge difference between buying lunch for your partner because you are terrified of what you think will happen if you don't (you will lose them), versus you wanting to buy your partner lunch because you know they love surprises and that will deepen the bond you have with them. Always look back to intention when trying to assess whether an attachment behavior was harmful or not. Is that behavior based out of fear or authenticity?

## Exercise: Identify Signs of Codependency

Now that you've learned the signs of codependency, reflect back on your relationships with yourself and others and see what you notice. Do not judge yourself for what happened in the past; simply make observations. Ask yourself these questions and practice radical self-honesty when answering them:

- If I were to place a boundary with a loved one, would any fears flow into my mind? (For example, "I'm scared they will hate me.")
  - If fear is present, is that fear based in abandonment, rejection, or being invalidated?
  - What other things may be behind that fear?
- Do I think love is a tally system? As in: If my partner does something for me, I owe them something back? Do I feel guilty if I don't find a way to repay them?
- Do I think that it's my responsibility to fix my partner's problems in their life (work, stress, emotional issues, family issues)?

- Do I think I'm selfish if I expect my partner to take an active role in their responsibilities?
- Does my partner think it's my responsibility to figure things out for them?
- Am I terrified of saying no to people?
- Am I uncomfortable making decisions on my own?
- When I make a decision, do I cross-check that decision with multiple people to ensure that my decision was correct?

Take a moment to review your answers and reflect on any patterns that connect to codependency, enmeshment, or people pleasing. Now reflect on your current perception of love:

- Does your current perception of love value your authenticity and your unique perspective?
- Does your current perception of love value your individual thoughts and desires?
- How does your current perception of love mirror the relationship (the bond) you currently have with yourself? (For example, if you think your partner only loves you because you are attractive, ask yourself, *Do I only think I have value because of the way I look?*)
- Do you use the tally system on yourself? (For example, "I can only eat dessert if I work out," or "I can only take a nap if I clean my entire room.")
- Does your self-love look like genuine kindness or is it contingent upon how strict, good, committed, or disciplined you are?

Your answers to these questions can indicate whether your perception of love includes your own needs and preferences.

## HEALING FROM CODEPENDENCY

The scenarios discussed so far in this chapter should help you understand just how problematic codependent tendencies are. You can easily lose your identity if you struggle with codependent traits and meet someone who is toxic and manipulative. You can also lose partners who *aren't* toxic because of the way your brain demands you to always read between the lines (due to past relationship trauma) and see problems that aren't there.

Toxic partners see codependency as a way to use your wounds against you. Healthy partners see a codependent partner as someone who struggles to show up to the relationship as their authentic self, and that confusion can cause a strain on the relationship as well.

## IT'S NOT YOUR FAULT

If any parts of your story sound like what we discussed in this chapter, understand that this is not your fault. You did not ask to be indoctrinated into an enmeshment ideology. You did not want to view relationships like this. You did not want to be manipulated. You did not ask to form this understanding of "love." *Love* is in quotations for a reason: This perception of love isn't love at all. It's weaponized connection.

If you are getting help now, what comes next will likely be better. When you are healing, you are getting to know yourself. You are unlearning harmful ideologies. You are learning what wounded perceptions you hold and how those perceptions embed themselves into your life. You are deconstructing your negative past concepts of "love" and rebuilding positive and healthy ones.

## YOUR PERCEPTIONS *CAN* CHANGE

If you have endured years of enmeshment, codependency, and/or manipulation, your view of love can become very distorted. Despite what codependency teaches, love is not something to leverage. Love is not something to be weaponized. Love—real, authentic love—is freely given and consensually received.

No matter how entrenched things feel now, your perceptions can change, norms can be challenged, and concepts can be reevaluated. You can experience healthy, genuine, and authentic love in the relationship you have with yourself and the relationships you have with others. It takes enormous amounts of self-reflection, self-compassion, and radical self-honesty to untangle all of this, but with every step you take, you are contributing to your own healing. You are moving forward in the direction of growth and expansion. Relating to people in a healthy way is hard work; being able to identify what love is and what love is not takes time, effort, and a considerable amount of energy. In this book, you are in the process of learning how to recover from a harmful relationship—and you are learning how to develop a deeply connected, radically honest, and authentic relationship with yourself.

## KEY TAKEAWAYS

- Identifying how enmeshment affects your intimate partnerships can help you start to unlearn harmful behaviors that were normalized for you.
- Enmeshed couples see individualization as selfish or a threat to the integrity of the relationship.
- People with codependency struggle with boundaries and a personal concept of their own identity and voice.
- Considerate couples balance their individual needs with the needs of their partner.
- Enmeshed/codependent partners solely focus on external needs, which builds an internalized resentment and feelings of self-rejection.
- Codependency and enmeshment are taught through patterns and are not something you brought upon yourself.

# CHAPTER 6

# HOW TOXIC RELATIONSHIPS CYCLE

Get together, fight, break up…then make up, get back together, and start over again. There are entire TV series featuring couples who cycle between getting together, fighting, having a passionate reconnection, and then suffering a vitriolic breakup. Then they repeat it all again the next season.

This cycle is not some weird fluke; it's a common part of toxic relationships. The cycle occurs because of the combination of conclusions, perceptions, and realities that are present in the relationship. In this chapter, you will learn important aspects of a toxic relationship breakup cycle. Within the cycle lies information that can be utilized during your healing. Let's break down the breakup cycle. But first—read the following section on breaking up safely.

## SAFETY FIRST!

**The following chapter is for people who are in a breakup cycle with individuals who are emotionally immature or exhibiting toxic traits but do *not* show any signs of being lethal or becoming violent.** If you are in a relationship with someone who has exhibited acts of violence or has the potential to become dangerous, breaking up with them can be unsafe or even sometimes deadly. The most dangerous time for a person breaking up with someone who is abusive is during the breakup phase.

If you are in a relationship where you feel there would be even a slight possibility that you would be in danger if you were to attempt to end the relationship, it is important to connect with local services that can help you create an escape plan to ensure a safe break from your partner. (See the Important Resources list at the end of the book to find support services that can assist with an action plan.)

If you are unsure if your partner might be violent in the event of a breakup, here are some risk factors to consider (content warning: reading through these may be disturbing).

### Risk Factors for Breakup Violence
- They are impulsive.
- They don't trust you or anyone else.
- They show signs of paranoia (in the past or currently).
- They don't have close bonds with others (family or friends).
- They have intense mood swings.
- They lack empathy.
- They exploit or manipulate others for personal gain.
- They engage in frequent acts of revenge.
- They show high levels of aggression.
- They lack remorse.
- They show pleasure from cruelty (emotional or physical).
- They show little or no accountability for their actions (and if they do show accountability, it's to get people to side with them, not because they truly are holding themselves accountable).
- They have said that they own you, your children, and/or your life.
- They are possessive over you, your time, your money, your things, and your relationships.
- They have intense pride and they see their relationship with you as an image to maintain (therefore, breaking up would injure their ego).
- They have physically abused you in the past (choking, shaking, slapping, punching, pushing).

- They have threatened to abuse you.
- They have threatened your life or their own.
- There is a weapon in the home.
- They have pulled a weapon on you or threatened to.
- They have forced you to do sexual acts, and they may have threatened you or another person's life (for example, your children) if you didn't comply with their demands.
- They have injured or killed a family pet or an animal on purpose.
- They have a substance use disorder that is unmanaged.
- They have full control over finances and/or have financially abused you.
- There is a significant amount of money or assets that will be lost if the relationship ends.

Lastly, there are certain comments a potentially violent partner might make. Here are some red flag phrases to listen for:

- "I'll never let you leave."
- "I'll die before you break up this family."
- "I'll take us both out if I have to."
- "It's not rape because we are married."
- "I will kill you before you get a chance to leave."
- "If you leave, I'll kill your ___ [dog/kid/mom/sister/etc.]."
- "You deserve everything that's coming to you."
- "Why do you make me hurt you?"
- "Why do you make me say things like this?"

Remember, your partner does not have to check every bullet on this list. After an abusive relationship, it's easy to tell ourselves, "Well, they aren't like that *all* the time" or "That just happened a few times." One threat is enough. One threat is one too many.

If your partner aligns with even *some* of these characteristics, breaking up with them can be dangerous. Please do not break up with them alone or impulsively. A plan must be created to keep you as safe as possible. The sad truth is: For some, breaking up while remaining safe is a privilege. If you are in a place where you think you may need to create a plan of action for breaking up safely, please utilize the resources found at the end of this book and know that it's better to be wrong about predicting their potential for danger and be safe than the alternative. Plus, even if nothing happens, it doesn't necessarily mean you were wrong about them—it may just mean you created a plan that they found harder to disrupt.

---

### Don't Practice Abuser Aligning

If you know someone who was physically injured or killed after a breakup, this does not mean those individuals weren't "smart enough" or didn't create a good enough escape plan. Violence and homicide are 100 percent the abuser's fault. They took it upon themselves to harm an individual. Blaming the victim is never okay.

---

## DECIDING TO BREAK UP

Once you have decided you are in a place where it is safe for you to think about ending your toxic relationship, consider for a moment what factors went into your decision to break up. Maybe you went to therapy, consulted friend groups, did research online about harmful relationship tactics, got advice from a trusted coworker, or listened to a podcast that motivated you to make a change. What has to happen in order for a breakup to occur? The relationship has to become so uncomfortable, so unstable, and so disruptive to your inner self that your mind says, "This isn't worth it." You decided that in order to really heal and focus on your own personal growth, you need to end the relationship. With that breakup comes inevitable complications.

## KNOWN AND UNKNOWN

In Chapter 5, you learned about codependency. Many relationships that experience the "on-again, off-again" dynamic have codependency issues. Codependency can create an inaccurate assumption about the way a "typical" relationship "should" function. It can be easy to normalize traumatic events, manipulative behaviors, and neglectful partners once they are known and predictable experiences for you.

During the first breakup, however, you enter unknown territory. You are now entering into a situation where you have to let go of the familiar and that can be very scary. What you do in this unknown typically determines whether the relationship will cycle back into itself.

### Leaving Is Complicated

When you leave a relationship, you leave more than just a person—you leave an idea, a hope, and an investment. You leave future memories you wanted to create, goals you wanted to accomplish together, and maybe even the home you shared. You leave the familiar. The familiar is *very* powerful. Everyone yearns for the familiar, even if it's painful. We like to have things known, and we will usually choose the known over the unknown.

## CULTURAL AND FINANCIAL CONSIDERATIONS

Relationships exist across every culture, ethnicity, and socioeconomic status. Because of that, leaving relationships may be harder or easier depending on the cultural considerations that surround the individuals in the relationship. Consider these common scenarios:

- **Financial considerations:** A partner who has no credit was unable to cosign for the down payment of the house that they lived in with their partner. This partner stayed at home raising the children they had together and thus has no job history. They may choose to stay with their abusive partner because they will be homeless without a way to get a new place easily if they break up.

- **Cultural and religious values:** If a culture or religion teaches individuals to value commitment above all else, a partner in an abusive relationship will feel trapped and might even feel like it's dishonorable to end the relationship.

- **Healthy relationship privilege:** If you've never experienced a toxic relationship, you've been privileged to enjoy healthy relationships, even if they weren't perfect. It might be very difficult for you to understand why someone "can't just leave" or even why someone would return to a relationship that was abusive in the past. If you have never experienced manipulation at the hands of a partner or been threatened with violence by your partner, if you never had your children weaponized against you, or thought you might lose your dog because your partner threatened to kill the dog if you break up, it will not make sense to you why some people end up staying in a relationship that hurts them so much. The truth is, people stay not because they aren't smart enough or aware enough—they stay because of multiple considerations that collectively influence that decision. Sometimes it's the threat of violence but other times it can be harder to see, like family values around divorce or complex financial issues. So if you haven't been in this position yourself, know that breakups aren't just as simple as leaving if things get hard. There are deep and nuanced layers that you may not understand.

## WHAT DAY ONE FEELS LIKE

The first day of the breakup is so important. That freedom you feel? It's real. That relief you have in your chest? It's real. That sadness you feel because you really did care about them? That's real too. The tricky part is that all of the wounds you have don't just magically heal on day one.

## FEAR SETS IN

Even if you initially feel relieved and happy, you still may be terrified of ending up alone. You might be afraid that you'll never find love again. You might be scared no one will want you or ever care about you again. Your ex may even be telling you those narratives to plant seeds of fear in you. These fears are also real, and if left unprocessed, can be a powerful force that contributes to people getting back together with their ex.

### Revisit the Both/And Concept

When you experience a fear about being alone after you break up with a toxic partner, take a moment and remember the both/and mentality from Chapter 1. Remember, the both/and mindset allows you to feel two things at the same time. You are allowed to be both relieved the relationship is over and sad that it is. Acknowledging and accepting both feelings can protect you from making impulsive decisions about entering back into a toxic relationship. Holding two truths at the same time gives your mind space to heal without having to label or force a certain feeling. You have achieved the both/and mindset when you are able to think things like: *I can miss my partner and realize that they are not mentally healthy enough to be in a relationship with. I can love my partner and realize that the way they love me is harming me.*

## THE LABELING TRAP

The human mind prefers that every thought is assigned a nice, neat category. It wants to label feeling one way or another. During a breakup, labeling might look like making lists of "reasons I shouldn't take them back" or "reasons we should get back together." What's really going on there is a push for an all-or-nothing fallacy (also discussed in Chapter 1). Your mind then gets to work labeling every thought, emotion, or memory as evidence for or against the ending of the relationship. The problem is, this is the most biased jury you have ever met! You might have a hundred reasons why you *shouldn't* get back together with them, but because your mind (the jury) is in an all-or-nothing mindset, that handful of reasons why the relationship could work might overrule (thanks, for example, to your fears of being alone) and tell you, "You must have come to the wrong conclusion; we need to get back together!!"

It's both. You have reasons why you should remain broken up and reasons why you could get back together. Reassure your mind that it's okay to feel both, so it doesn't feel like you have to choose.

## ELEMENTS OF THE BREAKUP CYCLE

When you take a step back and examine how toxic relationships cycle after a breakup, certain themes become clear. In this section, you will learn about a few core elements that contribute to the breakup cycle—specifically, the wounds that were carried into the relationships or were formed during the relationship, perceptions of blame, and distortions of responsibility.

Take a moment and bring in compassion for yourself; know that by identifying the elements found within a breakup cycle you are gaining traction in your healing, and establishing a footing to stand on when attempting to navigate elements and perceptions that may need to be challenged in the future.

### WHAT ARE RELATIONAL WOUNDS?

Relational wounds are faulty constructs that shape your conceptualizations of what a relationship should feel like or be like, what is deemed acceptable or tolerable, and what is normalized. Collectively, they are the components of relational trauma. The wounds were either brought in from previous relationships or developed inside of the relationship you are attempting to leave or remain separate from.

Here is what relational wounds might sound like:

- "I can't complain about an issue in our relationship because if I do, I will seem ungrateful for the things they do for our relationship." (This is the all-or-nothing thinking we discussed in Chapter 1.)
- "I have to just accept them the way they are, because if I bring up a concern about their behavior or a concern about their lack of engagement in the relationship, then I am being judgmental. I don't want them to judge me, so how can I judge them?"
- "I can't ask for what I want because then I'm being selfish."
- "A relationship is all about giving. It's all right if giving hurts, is painful, or is so self-sacrificing that I lose myself completely. All that means is that I am truly devoted to them, and that's good!"
- "A relationship is about going with the flow, so I usually follow their lead, and allow them to direct everything."
- "Sometimes it's easier to stay quiet and keep the peace."
- "I let my partner's vision of our relationship take precedence over mine."

What's lacking in all of the statements in this list is the both/and mindset. You are in a relationship both with your partner and with yourself. If you neglect the relationship you have with yourself and instead always choose your partner, you're exhibiting a deep relational wound. Partners with fewer emotional skills often resort to tactics like encouraging partners to feel guilt, shame, and/or judged in order to establish the relationship *they* want.

## Case Study: How Relational Wounds Can Form

Dan had told Nora in the beginning of their relationship that once a week he goes to his buddy's house to play cards. When Dan goes to leave for one of those game nights, Nora says, "You are really going to leave again for your stupid game night?" Dan is confused and says, "Nora, it's not stupid to me. This has been a tradition that I've had with my friend since high school—it's actually the only reason I have been able to maintain these friendships for so long." Nora scoffs and says, "Whatever, just go."

Dan feels trapped. He feels like he can't go because Nora will be mad but he also is confused because he explicitly explained to Nora that this event was important to him. Dan prompts one more time, "Nora, if you are upset, I'd want to talk about your frustration." Nora quickly replies, "Ugh, forget it! Just go and be selfish like you always are." As the weeks go by, Dan starts feeling really selfish and guilty about going to game night. Eventually he stops going, and now he rarely sees his buddies. When he does see them, he feels an immense sense of guilt.

The relational wound in this example is the construct of selfishness. Dan is being taught that having time for himself to develop and nurture relationships outside of his relationship with his partner is wrong. In this example, Nora seems to perceive any outside relationship as a threat and she is teaching Dan to create that construct inside of himself.

Dan realized he was losing touch with his family and friends and his entire life was revolving around Nora, and the two break up. Even though Nora and Dan are no longer together, the relational wound is still there. Dan will need to contend with the relational wound that resulted from being told he was selfish for taking time for himself and his relationships.

## SELF-BLAME

Blaming the self and taking full responsibility for a relationship breakdown is another culprit in the cycle. Toxic partners teach you to be overly responsible for their needs. The partner who is toxic will work hard to develop a pattern of belief that you are the reason for all of their problems. In their mind, if you have the audacity to consider your needs, vision, wants, and desires, then *you are the problem.*

Blaming yourself and coming to the conclusion that you are the full extent of the problem is a relational wound. The idea that being treated well is a luxury that you don't deserve in a relationship was cultivated from a partner who benefited from you neglecting yourself. Read that again if you need to! This dynamic plays into the breakup cycle because if your partner has convinced you that you don't get to take care of yourself, breaking up with them is going to be seen as you being selfish.

*The idea that being treated well is a luxury that you don't deserve in a relationship was cultivated from a partner who benefited from you neglecting yourself.*

## SHIFTING RESPONSIBILITY

Cyclical relationships have themes. Typically, there is one party who is attempting to ask difficult questions, encourage growth, and foster change, while the other party is calling that effort dramatic, overbearing, or overzealous. If your partner is frustrated by your efforts to recognize issues in the relationship, they might be trying to shift responsibility for their issues back onto you. You might hear phrases like:

- "Why do you always have to point out the negative?"
- "Why can't you just get over it?"
- "Why are you hassling me with this?"
- "It's always *something* with you."

Playing the cycle out, the partner who wants to grow will often get fed up, end things, but then immediately doubt that choice. That doubt might even lead to that partner calling their ex and apologizing for dwelling on the past. The ex happily agrees that the partner who wanted a more healthy dynamic was wrong for having that expectation and the ex accepts them back.

The toxic partner doesn't see the need to gain new relationship skills or emotional regulation skills. They see any request for that to happen as "you not accepting them for who they are." In a toxic relationship:

- Awareness of the problem will be labeled as "judgmental" or "stirring the pot."
- Accountability will be labeled as "holding a grudge" or "making them feel guilty."
- Action steps toward change will be labeled as "too needy" or having "too high expectations."

The toxic partner will have you taking every class, reading every book, and going to every therapy appointment in an attempt to convince you that if you just changed that this relationship would work. But what they are really asking you to do is to allow them to remain unchecked while you try to develop coping skills around the obvious mental health fallout you are enduring for the amount of manipulation, gaslighting, and abuse that is occurring.

## Exercise: Reflect On Your Breakup

Think back to when your breakup occurred. Take a moment to identify wounds that started aching afterward, thoughts that starting spiraling, and doubts that slowly crept in.

- Name those wounds.
- Name those thoughts.
- Name those doubts.

Let's reflect: Which narrative(s) were the most compelling to you? If you did get back together, which narratives led you back into the relationship? Which narratives eventually convinced you to try to amend the relationship, one more time? By looking at the reflection points you came up with, you can see more clearly the themes that presented in your particular relationship that compelled you to "try again."

## BUT I WANT THEM BACK!

All this talk of breakup cycles and relational wounds can start to feel a little clinical. Let's bring in some humanity here. You may have spent years with this person—of course you miss them! Judging yourself for missing them is going to damage the relationship you have with yourself. You are allowed to miss them without immediately running back into their arms. (There's the mixed feeling concept again—remember, both things can be true.)

Healing from a toxic relationship means you need to be radically honest with yourself. Ask yourself hard questions, like:

- Is this truly what I think love feels like?
- Is this relationship mimicking the relationship I had with my parents or grandparents growing up (the people who taught me how to give and receive love)? Do I *want* that?
- Is this love, or is it a familiar cycle of seeking out fulfillment from someone who manipulates me?
- Am I being shamed for wanting more?

Your answers to these questions can help you separate the person from the relationship for a moment and assess whether the relationship itself was what you wanted.

# KEY TAKEAWAYS

- Leaving relationships can be dangerous. Review behaviors and patterns of your partner before considering a plan of action for breaking up.
- Breaking up is complicated and there are multiple factors that go into an "on-again, off-again" relationship.
- Labeling everything after a breakup as good or bad, amazing or terrible fuels the counterproductive all-or-nothing belief system. Instead, use the both/and mentality to protect your mind from falling into thinking traps.
- When the mind quiets after a breakup, the temptation to go back and self-doubt creep in.
- Identifying relational wounds can help untangle the confusion between what is healthy and what is familiar in a relationship.
- Blaming yourself and taking on all of the mental load and emotional labor for the relationship is unhealthy and fuels the belief that you are the problem.
- Humanizing your feelings after a breakup is important, but missing your ex and needing to get back together are not the same thing.

# CHAPTER 7

# STEP INTO YOUR POWER

*You are responsible for your own healing.* Think about this statement. Some people with a past traumatic relationship might feel uncomfortable hearing this fact because it can come off as uncompassionate or even cruel, especially if someone is struggling to connect the dots in their healing journey. But the key is to use that statement to empower yourself, not cause fear or doubt. In your toxic relationship, you may not have been able to make independent decisions, follow your dreams, or live as your authentic self. Now that you are healing, you can take control of your life, maybe even for the first time. That power might feel unusual and intimidating at first, but as you learn and grow, you can come to cherish that power.

No more looping, no more cycling—the relationship has finally reached its end. So what now?

Well, it will be very tempting to jump into the next relationship, but this is a defining moment for you so take your time and reflect. You have spent the last several chapters looking back into your toxic relationship to learn what happened and why. Now we'll begin to turn the page and look forward to your future—one where your needs, preferences, and rights are front and center. In this chapter, you'll prepare yourself to move forward with healing and learn a healing modality that I created called the OASIS model. This model will provide a structure for your healing and give you key touchpoints to return to as you move along your healing journey.

## CHALLENGING "STINGS"

As you begin to turn your attention toward your healing, it's helpful to focus on painful points to help identify the areas you'll want to focus on first. Leading with curiosity, start wondering about times when a kind word, idea, situation, or statement stings. Saying that something "stings" refers to that feeling when someone tells you something that is meant to build you up or genuinely be nourishing to your psyche—but you immediately refute or downplay it. Statements like "You are a gift," "You are really strong," or "You are so kind" seem like they'd be welcomed—but if you're recovering from a toxic relationship, you may have a different reaction. If what enters your mind looks counter to the kind point, that is a sign there is more to explore. Continuing to stay nonjudgmental and curious, you would ask yourself, *Why does it sting when someone tells me I am kind?*

Challenging these "stings" can help you sway your thoughts and differentiate your true authentic voice from the trauma voice. For example, if someone says, "You are so kind," and you say, "Well, I don't feel comfortable with you saying that because I'm not *always* kind," you are revealing your perception of yourself. Your thinking pattern is anchored in an all-or-nothing narrative—and that narrative is a very distorted version of reality. As you move forward with your healing, try to be aware of these stings so you can explore the thematic depth of them (see Chapter 1) to see what's under your discomfort.

### Are You the "Common Denominator"?

When relationships that occur after the toxic relationship start to go south, you might start to think you are the main reason all the relationships you have fail. Some people even label themselves the "common denominator." In truth, though, the only common denominators that are present are painful, inaccurate, and harmful perceptions of love and belonging. Those common denominators are not you! They are the indoctrinated thoughts that were woven deep into your psyche while you were conceptualizing your understanding of how to give and receive love. Unlearning these thoughts is essential for healing.

## AVOID CRITICAL TEACHERS

As you begin to focus on your healing, you want to create an environment that's conducive to learning and growing. Think about when you first entered school. In order to create an environment for learning, you needed to be curious, keep an open mind, and feel safe asking questions.

> ### Be Curious
>
> One strategy to begin healing wounds from a toxic relationship is starting with curiosity. Ask yourself the meaning behind any hesitation, pain, lack of compassion for your emotions, or any other tension points that show up in everyday life. Curiosity will elicit much greater growth than just hyperfocusing on individual pain points. Revisit the discussion of thematic depth in Chapter 1 with these reflections. Expand the thought out to a broader view and examine it through themes. Once you are able to identify themes of thinking, you can target the source and prompt some transformative growth.

When you are doing healing work, you must create an environment within and around yourself that nourishes you. Your past toxic relationships promoted environments that were just the opposite, so you'll need to make active choices to think and do things differently. Just like that student in school, you'll want to be curious, keep an open mind, and ask questions. This goal can be easier said than done, though, because many people hear a very cruel voice when they start to reflect. This voice is like a merciless and critical teacher. Think about the learning environment that your least favorite teacher growing up created. You might have been scared, upset, angry, or confused in that class. If you have spent years with a "cruel teacher," they've influenced your inner narrative and the way your internal voice sounds. This cruel teacher may have started off as a parent, then a partner, and then maybe it became you.

## Case Study: The Power of Processing

Kelly is finally through the thick of it. She went back and forth with her ex, Mark, and now it's clear: They are officially over. Kelly wishes she could just find someone new, because then at least she wouldn't have to feel so alone. She immediately downloads dating apps to try to distract herself from the pain of the breakup.

She talks to a few new people, but realizes on those dates she is still very much struggling and feeling conflicted: She feels guilty for feeling good about being rid of Mark and she feels relieved that the relationship is finally over. Yet, she also feels bad that she misses him. Kelly finds herself talking about Mark during the few dates she has had. She feels torn all the time. She concludes that because she misses him, she must want Mark back.

After reflecting for a bit on that thought, though, she tells herself, "No, I don't want Mark, I just want a partner—but someone without all those toxic traits." Kelly has learned the power of processing and time. Time with a thought can be scary, but with skills, that time gives you the opportunity to understand parts of yourself that you didn't previously have access to.

## MIND THE GAP

Having a gap of time between an old toxic relationship and entering a new one is important. This gap can be very informative or tormenting, depending on which strategies you apply. If you just continue old habits, you'll feel confused, conflicted, and uncomfortable. But if you try newer, healthier strategies and mindsets, you'll make progress—even if this progress is slow—toward healing. It is important to use this gap to breathe, reflect, and feel without the complexities of new love interests.

This gap doesn't have to last forever, of course. But while you're in it, think about what information can be gathered during the gap. What new skills can you learn? What traumatic perceptions can you reframe? Please note: If you are already in a new relationship, you are able to do all of this processing work as well; just keep in mind the way your new relationship may affect your processing of your old relationship.

## Exercise: Determine What Is Left Over from Your Previous Relationship

This exercise helps you appreciate the power of taking time for processing and encourages you to see the importance of mindfully connecting to past perceptions. Ask yourself these questions with radical honesty:

- What perceptions are lingering from my past relationship?
- What beliefs do I carry about myself now that I didn't have before my past relationship?
- What perceptions do I hold now that I didn't have before my past relationship?
- What were some things about my past relationship that I thought were normal while inside of the relationship, but upon exiting it, can now realize were harmful and untrue?
- How have I processed my emotions surrounding my past relationship?
- How did I cope with the ending of that relationship? What specific things did I do? (List them if you can.)

Review your list, and identify things that led you to develop a deeper relationship with yourself. Star those and celebrate your progress!

## INDIVIDUAL VERSUS COLLECTIVE HEALING

Did you know that healing is both an individual experience and a collective one? Here's how those two concepts are different:

- **Individual healing** is healing that occurs in personal, inner worlds, healing past perceptions, past beliefs, and past behaviors.

- **Collective healing** is healing that occurs in the environment around you. Collective healing happens when groups of people understand the oppressive and exploitative systems that surround them and refuse to normalize harmful procedures, policies, and practices in that system.

Perceiving healing as a solely individual experience is neglecting the fact that we exist in a sociological system, and perceiving it as solely a collective experience neglects the fact that we must individually bring our healing into the collective so the entire system can shift. It must be viewed as a co-occurring endeavor. Healing individually is as important as healing collectively.

The mistake so many people make is that they see someone else healing or view someone as mentally strong and think, *Oh, I'm attracted to that because I also want those skills*, when the truth of the matter is that your partner isn't your teacher, your therapist, or your mentor. Likewise, if a couple goes to couples therapy but does not go to individual therapy, they are trying to heal the collective without working on the individual. A partner can help you integrate and practice your own personal emotional skills, but they can't bear the responsibility of educating and establishing new skill development.

## EMOTIONAL PIGGYBACKING

If your partner has very few emotional skills and you attempt to start healing by going to therapy, learning new ways to communicate, and expanding your perception with exposure to psychologically rich communities and learning environments, a discrepancy between your skills and your partner's skills can become apparent. *Emotional piggybacking* is a term that refers to situations when your partner sees your progression and expects you to teach them all you know and then acts as though they are healing by proxy. Another way to think about this is they are "stealing your healing." This looks like your partner provoking you by saying, "Well, now that you're the mental health expert, you tell me what I'm doing wrong!" I'm proposing the term emotional piggybacking because it creates a visual for you that one partner is not doing any individual work; they are watching you do your own work and trying to appropriate your healing as theirs while you carry the emotional labor.

In a toxic dynamic, a partner may not realize they are emotionally piggybacking. Nonetheless, it's confusing for someone who is receiving messages from their partner that they are willing to listen and change and learn—but then just turn you into their therapist or their educator without shifting their behaviors or developing new skills.

## OWN YOUR POWER

Perhaps one of the most important themes to understand as you begin to focus on healing is that you are incredibly powerful. Think about what it would be like if a friend, parent, or therapist looked at you and said, "You are the source of your power. You are a force to be reckoned with. You are fierce. You are emboldened. You are strong!" Now consider how that would feel if those statements came from you—and you actually believed them.

Those words *are* true: You are the source of your own power. Think about that for a moment. Your power does not come from:

- Other people giving you a sense of power.
- Taking other people's power away.
- Other people affirming that your power is there.
- Other people giving you accolades for your power.

When your power is embodied, it is yours. Looking at yourself as a source of strength is a way to stabilize your recovery based on you, not others.

## Exercise: Repeat This Affirmation

Owning your power may not come naturally at first. To help you get more comfortable with this feeling, read through this long affirmation. Read it once for comprehension and then again, as many times as you like, so you can practice what embodying your own healing feels like.

"I was always worthy—but for years, my pain and trauma told me that I was not worthy of the freedom that healing brings. My trauma told me, *You are shackled by this and you'll stay shackled forever.* That is not true. I will work through this healing journey to reclaim sovereignty over my life, which belongs to no one other than me."

# THE OASIS MODEL

I developed the OASIS model to provide a structure for healing after trauma. It focuses on the layers of complex interactions that occur within the self, in the form of:

- **O**wnership (of self)
- **A**uthenticity
- **S**elf-Sovereignty
- **I**nterdependency
- **S**elf-Advocacy

In this book, I am applying the model to intimate relationships, but it is also applicable to all interpersonal relationships that have endured relational trauma. (You'll learn more about each of the OASIS components soon.) The model is based on integrated ideologies found in narrative, humanistic, and psychodynamic therapy.

## WHAT DOES THE OASIS MODEL DO?

Many healing modalities approach healing by bypassing the authority inside of the individual and instead placing it on another source—such as another person (perhaps a sponsor or a therapist), God or a religious authority figure (like a pastor or a priest), or even pop psychology self-help gurus. Yet, there is a huge difference between someone facilitating healing and someone being the one and only source of that healing. Because of that bypassing of personal owner-ship over recovery, the codependency wound is not healed; it's merely transferred to another source. In the OASIS model, you are the source. Your power is never transferred; it's affirmed within you. The OASIS model views you as someone who's wise, able, valued, and evolving. This model can help you:

- Build a healthy relationship within yourself.
- Deepen the bond you have with your internal voice.
- Show you how to navigate challenges in trauma recovery.
- Bolster self-trust and self-conviction.
- Cultivate a firm sense of self-governance.
- Help you experience your own power without manipulating others to gain that feeling.

*In the OASIS model, you are the source of your power. Your power is never transferred; it's affirmed within you. The OASIS model views you as someone who's wise, able, valued, and evolving.*

## SELF-OWNERSHIP

Ownership of self, or self-ownership, is the first component of the OASIS model for healing. This is the idea that not only are you allowed to be your own individual; you *must* be. Self-ownership looks like own-ing your narrative and your subsequent choices. Self-ownership at its core is about the relationship you have with your own power; it helps heal the wound that says, "You don't have power over anything" and "You are your failures."

Owning your life can be overwhelming. When you fully own your life, you own every part of it. You own the reactions, the trau-mas, the pleasure, and the pain. Was that trauma your fault? No. Did the reaction you had during that trauma response hurt someone you loved? Possibly.

Let's say you scream at your friend to shut up because she started laughing really loudly at a restaurant. You struggle with loud noises because your ex used to yell very loudly at you all the time. This is a moment where two things are coexisting: Your past trauma showed up and caused a ripple effect on your relationships. You just experienced a trauma response and your friend is validly upset that she was scolded like a child. If you acknowledge her emotions *and* your emotions—as not being in competition with each other—that's self-ownership.

Self-ownership is not about shame; it's about honoring the complexities of your trauma and how that trauma shows up. It's about compassionate consideration of how your trauma affects your everyday life and at times how that trauma can affect other people. Relationships thrive when people embody self-ownership. When someone can acknowledge how their hard day is bleeding into another person's, that is powerful. It shows a deep connection to introspection and represents a honed skill set around emotional processing.

## AUTHENTICITY

Authenticity in the OASIS model is a direct counter to the trauma brain's propensity to disregard your own needs and insert the needs or wants of another person. Authenticity counters that dismissal by amplifying your inner voice and helping that inner voice take action.

### Being Authentic Will Change Your Relationships

Some of your personal relationships will change when you "unmask," or stop pretending. Taking that mask off will make some people uncomfortable. Some of your friends and family will celebrate your authenticity, but others will reject you. This is a tough part of healing, but in the long run, you want to be surrounded by those who love you for who you really are.

Authenticity teaches you to tap into the way you feel before, during, and after certain situations. It also asks, Are you faking it? If so, why? When you start paying attention to the times you are pretending to be something you are not (in other words, when you put on a mask to make others happy), it slowly becomes more and more painful to "play your part." On the other side of that mask is someone who spent years being forced down and shut away. Authenticity says it's time to unmask and see the sun.

## Case Study: Bumps in the Authentic Road

Traci has been dating Miles for a few months and she just started really diving into her healing journey. She started asking those authenticity questions surrounding her life and her interests and her values. She is slowly realizing that she is actually bisexual. She starts opening up to Miles about it and Miles really doesn't know how to process it. He is unsure about how to proceed.

The people who care about you are allowed to have time to process transitions. Showing up authentically can have growing pains because you do not want to thwart people's autonomy nor have them thwart yours. People are allowed to leave if they can't handle your authentic truth. If Miles is uncomfortable dating someone who is bisexual, Traci does not have to guilt him for that reaction. He is allowed to have his own authentic feelings around dating someone who is bi and if he realizes he will be threatened by every single friend that Traci has, he needs to be honest with himself and come to some hard conclusions about what that means.

If Miles and Traci decide to break up, that can be difficult. But it's a better and more authentic option than Traci pretending she's not bi and Miles pretending he is okay with it when he is not. You don't want a partner who resents your authentic self. You want a partner who embraces and celebrates that authenticity.

Authenticity requires you to have deep compassion for yourself while you are in a period of growth. Self-growth is not a neat, straight line in the right direction. It really looks like making a decision, changing your mind, moving forward in a different direction, making another decision, negotiating a few new challenges…and so on.

It's rocky and it's part of the learning and growing process. Here is a quick cheat sheet to help you identify whether you're acting in a way that is authentic or masking who you really are.

| Authenticity | Masking |
| --- | --- |
| Feels light | Feels forced |
| Feels refreshing | Feels pressured |
| Feels aligned with your values | Feels fake |
| Feels safe | Feels tense |

## Beware of Transactional Love

Let's say you asked your partner to clean out the garage while you are clearing out the basement. You realize that they are probably going to expect you to have sex with them later. That's an example of transactional love. Just because someone does a chore does not mean you have to comply with any request they might have afterward. Authentic love, on the other hand, looks like you asked your partner to clean out the garage and they fully consented to that task, not expecting you to give them something in return. They cleaned out the garage because they know that was the right thing to do and they are a partner in household chores. They make the choice to do that task out of an authentic connection to the relationship with you, *not* out of a means to an end to get their needs satisfied. Authentic love doesn't have to keep tally about what tasks are completed, because both parties are genuinely contributing to the collective outcome. Both parties are tapping into the genuine love and kindness they have for the other partner.

## SELF-SOVEREIGNTY

Self-sovereignty in the OASIS model focuses on embracing your power and committing to exercise that power over your life and boundaries. By practicing self-sovereignty, you are directly countering the belief that other people have authority over you and you must submit to the person with the most overt power (this could look like religious leaders, family elders, or even other professionals who are uninformed about trauma). In order for self-sovereignty to not turn into selfish toxicity, the practice must be rooted in a deep connection with humanity and informed by conscious and considerate ideology.

When you practice self-sovereignty, you are honoring your own authority as well as the autonomy of the people around you. Boundaries come into play here. Your own authority drives the belief that your boundaries are valid, your conclusions are reasonable, and taking care of yourself is essential to your trauma healing. By trusting that your boundaries are valid, you will reinforce the belief that you are able to provide safe protections for your psyche. This builds self-trust and self-conviction.

### Self-Sovereign versus Self-Righteous

Self-sovereignty concerns the relationship you are having with yourself; it's not about having authority over others. You are not taking your convictions and forcing them on others. Self-righteous people, on the other hand, are attempting to force you to believe what they believe. Self-sovereign people know their truth and do not go out of their way to convince others that their own beliefs are the right ones. They allow the other person to have their own autonomy and beliefs.

A hallmark of self-sovereignty is allowing yourself to change your mind after making a decision or allowing yourself to challenge or question external authority (such as politicians, elders, supervisors). You are taking on the full helm of your emotional navigation system.

Navigating your emotions can be overwhelming in the beginning, because you may start to realize how often you were allowing others to dictate your truth. This hurts, but know that you are healing just by becoming aware of this situation.

## Case Study: Practicing Self-Navigation

Erin is starting to practice self-sovereignty. She and her boyfriend, Luke, are out to lunch. They sit down and Luke starts talking to the server: "She'll have French fries and I'll have the onion rings."

Past versions of Erin would have just let Luke order for her and ignored the spike of tension that happened in her chest when he did that. Now that Erin is starting to practice self-sovereignty, she listens to that tension and notices that it is related to her being spoken for. This awareness gives her the courage to speak up before the server goes away. "Luke, I don't want French fries today." Then, turning to the server, she says, "I'll take the nachos, thank you."

Luke immediately looks annoyed and says, "Wow, way to make me look like an idiot!" Erin is concerned at Luke's response and then says, "I'm ordering the food I want to eat. Is that a concern for you?" Luke retorts, "Well, I was just trying to do something nice!" Erin keeps calm and says, "I can see why trying to order for your girlfriend could be cute to some people, but I am most comfortable speaking for myself in situations like this." Luke now opens up a bit and shares, "Sorry. Honestly, I'm glad I know how you feel, because I was always expected to order for my ex and she got mad when I didn't memorize her order."

In the past, Erin would have just sat there and eaten the French fries and slowly built resentment for her partner's overreach. Erin stepping into her sovereignty is what helps to break the cycle of misunderstanding. Luke being able to share his past experiences is a promising indication of his emotional skills.

## Exercise: Assess Your Self-Sovereignty

These questions will help you assess how far along in learning about self-sovereignty you are at this point:

- Are you enthusiastically consenting to the events you attend, the experiences you have, or the people you hang out with—or are you doing things out of obligation?
- Is someone speaking over you often?
- Does anyone "tell you how you feel" about certain things?
- Do you allow yourself the chance to disagree with people who you view as "authority" (such as your partner, pastor, parent, or certain professionals)?

Your response to every single question might not indicate self-sovereignty yet, and that's okay. This is a process, and you should celebrate any steps you take toward owning your power.

## INTERDEPENDENCY

Interdependency, or mutual dependency, is the state of being dependent on another for *certain* needs. In the OASIS model, interdependency tends to the wound that says you have to lose your individuality when you enter into a relationship. I know what you might be thinking: *Dependency?! After all I endured in my last relationship? Why would that be part of my healing journey?* The important element to extract from interdependency is that humans exist sociologically. We are social creatures and to some degree we all thrive with some level of social interaction. Wanting to be loved is not weakness and it's not pathetic. Wanting to be liked by your friends is not sad; it's based on the fundamental values we have as human beings. At this point in your healing, you want to unlearn *dependency* as a bad word and relearn it through the lens of a healthy relationship.

With healthy interdependency, you are both an individual in a relationship with yourself and a partner in a relationship with another person. You are in a both/and situation. Interdependent relationships highly value both the uniqueness of the individuals in the relationship and the shared entity that is formed by both partners coming together.

Here are some interdependent traits to look for in a potential partner:

- They say what they mean.
- They value your individuality (what makes you unique from them).
- They don't see your differences as a threat.
- They don't expect you to be their healer, problem solver, therapist, or decision maker.
- They honor your autonomy.
- They don't immediately agree with you on everything and hold their own opinion as valid without belittling you for having a difference of opinion.
- They strongly want you to be as authentic as possible.
- They want to learn how to navigate around your differences.

Interdependency is filled with mutual compassion, mutual discernment, mutual growth, and mutual pattern recognition. Remember, you are allowed to have needs. You are also allowed to ask your partner to compromise when differences arise. No one deserves to be in a relationship where you are constantly losing touch with who you really are.

The reason interdependency is so hard is because it takes two very attuned and engaged individuals to honor each other's differences and work together to create strategies that don't hinder either person's authenticity. When done right, interdependency helps heal relational wounds by showing you that it's possible for people to work through issues in a healthy way without anyone being robbed of their own autonomy. Interdependency cultivates hope, genuine connection, clear communication, and mutual trust.

# Exercise: Determine If Your Relationship Is Codependent or Interdependent

This exercise could be challenging because your partner will also need to have at least a basic level of self-awareness skills to start this work. If you don't have a partner at the moment, you can ask these questions with psychologically safe friends or family.

- Look for signs of psychological safety:
  - Do they get reactive when you bring up something difficult to discuss?
  - Do they allow you to feel your emotions without inserting a narrative over those emotions?
  - Are they using jokes so as to mock you or make under-handed comments?
  - Are they sarcastic and then say things like, "C'mon, I didn't mean it"?
  - Are they passive-aggressive?
  - Do they communicate their needs clearly?
- Look for signs of codependency:
  - Do they think that their problems are your problems and your problems are theirs to solve?
  - Do they partake in self-martyrdom? For example, they purposefully take on too much, like a project or a party, and then they get upset when people aren't helping enough.
  - Do they sacrifice things for you in the relationship but do so without authentically wanting to sacrifice those things? For example, they agree to stop eating meat because you went vegetarian but they make your life a living hell and com-plain every day about how much they miss meat.

## SELF-ADVOCACY

Self-advocacy tends to the wound that was formed when you were not able to speak up for yourself in the past. It is the last point on the OASIS model because it is healing in action. This is where the application of self-ownership, authenticity, self-sovereignty, and interdependence comes in. Taking everything you have learned and bringing those concepts into your lived reality is self-advocacy.

---

### A Note about Safety

Stepping into your power can be perceived as a threat to some individuals. Please use caution when practicing self-advocacy, and if you think you may not be safe advocating for yourself in an argument, choose safety first. Please see Important Resources at the back of the book for a list of resources surrounding this topic.

---

Speaking up for yourself takes a deep understanding of the way you deserve to be treated. Unfortunately, this understanding was impacted by your trauma. The brain that's experienced trauma convinces you that you aren't skilled enough to defend yourself, which leaves you without well-developed self-advocacy skills. Self-advocacy is so important to trauma healing because it helps your brain relearn that you *are* indeed capable. In practicing self-advocacy, your brain starts remembering that you are able to stand up for yourself. This builds immense self-trust the more it is practiced.

Starting to practice self-advocacy means fully connecting with your values. Especially the values found in the OASIS model:

- Do you believe that you are allowed to own your story and actions?
- Do you believe that you deserve to live as your authentic self?
- Do you acknowledge your own authority and sovereignty over your life?
- Do you seek interdependent friendships and partnerships?

When you become firm in these values, it will start to become painful to *not* advocate for yourself.

Moments for practicing self-advocacy surround you every day. Many people with histories of toxic relationships are scared to speak up for themselves because they don't want to be a bother. But remember, your brain takes note every time you bypass an opportunity to show up for yourself. You aren't being an inconvenience when you honor yourself. You are being present and kind by developing skills that deepen the relationship you have with yourself.

## Exercise: Practice Self-Advocacy

You can find everyday ways to work on your self-advocacy. That doesn't mean these ideas will immediately be simple to execute; but, like any skill, the more often you practice, the easier it'll become.

- Share your opinion on a hot topic with friends and practice using your voice and sharing your authentic values.
- Clarify how your name is pronounced if you have a name that is often said incorrectly.
- If a restaurant gets your order wrong, politely explain what you ordered to the server.
- If your parents disagree with you on a topic, practice standing in your truth while acknowledging they are allowed to hold a different opinion.
- If a partner is unkind during an argument, practice explaining how that behavior impacted you.

## LET OASIS LEAD YOU TOWARD HEALING

After enduring years of relational trauma, many people don't fully understand how to view themselves. The OASIS model is based on the idea that cultivating new perceptions about yourself and your relationships can radically shift your trajectory of healing. Deepening the relationship with yourself also provides a stabilization that many people recovering from toxic relationships long for.

When you are struggling with processing your relationship trauma, review the components of OASIS and allow the individual elements to guide your perceptions into a more stabilized understanding of the situation. OASIS will also be useful to you throughout the rest of this book. As you continue into Part 2, you will develop a vision for your future, strengthen your inner voice, and deepen your personal convictions—all of which build self-trust. OASIS focuses on deepening the connection and trust you have with yourself; that's how you'll shift deeply rooted concepts that were formed in trauma.

These conceptualizations are not formed overnight; it will take time. It will also take a lot of work, but it's the best kind of work because on the other side of this work is the self you fought to become.

## KEY TAKEAWAYS

- The OASIS model helps people engage with themselves in a new way during their trauma recovery and fosters self-trust.
- Self-ownership is tending to the perception of your story and the relationship you have with your own trauma.
- Authenticity is tending to the perception you have of your true self and whether you feel safe enough to express it.
- Self-sovereignty is tending to the perception you have of your own power and the authority you have over yourself.
- Interdependency is tending to the perception you have inside of an active relationship and how to mutually integrate that relationship into your life without losing the self.
- Self-advocacy is activating all of the previous concepts into your lived reality and standing strong in your newfound values.

# PART 2

# HEALING YOUR RELATIONSHIP WITH YOURSELF

The most important relationship you will ever cultivate is the relationship you have with yourself. The way you interact with your thoughts, wants, needs, and desires plays a huge part in how your everyday life is going to feel.

Just like any new relationship, it takes patience, effort, and commitment to develop a deep connection with yourself. This will take time and that's okay. Slow growth is sustainable growth. You will need to learn how to trust yourself, communicate kindly with yourself, and be patient with yourself during this journey. You will be unlearning and relearning how to interact with your mind.

Your authentic self has been waiting for you to arrive to this moment your entire life. Your true voice lies deep within you; it always has. Underneath the wounds and the trauma and the pain, you are there. It's time for you to step into the sun and feel your self-generated power for the very first time.

Be present in this moment. Take a deep breath, and visualize the images in the following passage as you read them:

Picture yourself approaching you. The person that is standing in front of you is a version of you that is fully embodied and fully empowered. You walk closer and you see the conviction in your eyes. You are grounded in your truth. You are guiding yourself for the first time in your life. No one is dictating your truth, your narrative, or your value. You can trust yourself now. You can sense how wise you have become. You even look different! Your posture, your stance, and the way you show up in this room takes your breath away. I'm not referring to beauty here; I'm referring to the energy you radiate now. Even the way you talk sounds different to you. There is passion in your voice. There is belief in your words. There is stability in your steps and you realize, as this version of you goes to place their hand on your shoulder, that you have become exactly who you've been waiting for in every partner you've ever wanted. You've become someone who loves themselves, deeply, without contingencies, caveats, or coercion.

This vision is what you are developing in reality via your healing. With each chapter, you are walking closer toward this version of yourself. You are strengthening yourself and building skills that are meant to radically shift the relationship you have with your current self. When that relationship starts to shift, you will feel it.

# CHAPTER 8

# CREATE YOUR VISION

Who are you as an individual? If I asked you to define yourself without a relational label (as in, parent, nurse, aunt, uncle, student, friend), how would you answer? Because you are developing the both/and mentality, it is important to think about how you are *both* an individual *and* someone actively in relationships with others. It's common in everyday life to define yourself by who you are in relation to others; you are also in a relationship with yourself and it's important to capture that identity too. When you are deeply connected with yourself, you'll find it's easier to bring your most authentic self to other relationships as well. In this chapter, you'll focus on entering into a new healthy relationship: the relationship with yourself.

## BUILDING A RELATIONSHIP WITHIN

Think about how you build relationships. Many times, they are relationships of convenience or happenstance—maybe you met someone at school and casually became friends over time. Or maybe you're a bartender who strikes up a conversation with a person you later start dating. Others scroll through dating apps and meet someone who seems to be interesting enough and hit it off.

Some of these relationships were probably developed with intention and you held a vision for where that relationship was going. Yet, many relationships don't have this vision. In this chapter, you'll create a vision for the relationship you have with yourself—one that is detailed, refined, and mindfully crafted.

## Affirmations That Are Helpful in Vision Work

The following affirmations might help you as you imagine your new vision for yourself. You can repeat them daily for motivation or to help you during a particularly challenging moment. See if any resonate with you, and feel free to change them as needed to speak directly to you.

- Looking into my past and dwelling on the past are two different things.
- I am clarifying my vision. This can feel painful *and* it will lead to peace.
- I am allowing my past pain to inform my future healing.
- I am getting to know my wounds for the first time and that is part of the healing process.
- With every emotion I hold and pain I process, I am deepening the relationship I have with myself.

## SOMETIMES YOU HAVE TO LOOK BACK

Vision work is partly about thinking about the path in front of you—and partly about examining the path you just walked down. It's tempting (and understandable) to want to forget your past trauma immediately and insist "I won't look back!" Yet, if you ignore where you've been, it's almost impossible to heal from it. You don't have to set your previous path on fire to heal. It is important, however, to explore that pain in order to mine nuggets of wisdom from it. Within your pain lies the information your brain needs to untangle beliefs, traumas, and automatic reactions that you unknowingly brought along for the ride. It's ideal for your new vision of yourself to be free of these past narratives, and identifying them will help you reimagine them.

## WHEN YOU DON'T EVEN KNOW WHERE TO START

You might be thinking, *I don't even know who I am anymore; how am I supposed to create a vision for who I want to be?!*

This mindset is unfortunately a common experience for many people exiting a harmful dynamic. They are left feeling lost, destabilized, decentered, and floundering. If you've spent years with a person who didn't allow you to develop your authentic self, it's difficult to even imagine what you could become. The following exercise is a really helpful place to start.

### Exercise: Remember a Happy Memory

For this exercise, you're going to look inward to a powerful happy memory you have.

- When was the last time you felt fully alive? Describe that moment.
- What exactly was happening?
- Who were you with?
- What emotions did you feel?
- What was the environment like? Try to use the five senses to give the description lots of richness. What did you smell, hear, taste, and so on?

Moments when we feel fully present and alive are captured in our memories for a reason. When your internal needs match your external environment, you feel alive and happy. You can then use your responses to these questions to help guide the vision you're creating for yourself. For example, if you answered that you felt most alive when you were out in nature, you might want to create a vision around connecting to the energy you find in nature.

## MAKE YOUR VISION SPECIFIC

Reread the visualization exercise at the beginning of Part 2. See how it is specific, positive, and assumes a healthy level of self-confidence? That's what you're going for. What you think about now doesn't have to be that long, but try to craft a goal that's reminiscent of that visualization.

The more specific you envision your relationship with yourself, the better. Some people start with a vague idea like: "I just don't want to hate myself anymore" (a statement that also comes from a place of deficit, not abundance). If you find yourself saying vague, negative statements like that, try reframing it into something like: "I want to deepen my connection with myself and change the way I speak to myself internally when I am facing a challenge."

---

### Use Your Vision to Set Goals

The energy you are tapping into as you create your vision can also lead to a specific goal or aim that deepens your bond with yourself. So, taking the nature example from the Remember a Happy Memory exercise, a small goal would look like: "I am going to spend twenty minutes outside by myself once a week." Starting small and taking tiny steps is key here. You should look forward to achieving these goals. You're more likely to maintain sustainable growth when you make incremental progress and ensure each goal is something that makes you feel happy and authentically *you*.

---

If your healing statements are vague and your emotional wounds are specific, you are not setting yourself up to be successful. You are attempting to heal, which is admirable, but the vision you have for that healing isn't structured in a way that promotes self-growth and self-exploration. The tone of your vision is important. Give yourself encouragement, compassion, and gentle understanding.

## FOCUS ON ABUNDANCE

As you create your vision, think about yourself from a place of abundance and what you *will* have or do (for example, *I will celebrate my successes*), not what you *won't* have or do (for example, *I'll stop being so hard on myself*). Focusing on what you lack is called "deficit mindset."

A deficit mindset can technically get the job done (you might have heard this type of talk from sports coaches trying to motivate athletes, maybe saying something like: "You certainly won't win if you keep playing that badly!"), but it does damage along the way. In self-work like the healing you are doing from a toxic relationship, focusing on the negative or deficits can block or destroy the new, healthier patterns you are trying to build.

*In self-work like the healing you are doing from a toxic relationship, focusing on the negative or deficits can block or destroy the new, healthier patterns you are trying to build.*

## Exercise: Respond to These Prompts to Help You Build Your Vision

This is a structure to help guide you as you start to build a vision of your future self. Starting is the hardest step, but these questions, affirmations, and prompts can help you get in the right frame of mind and jump-start your creativity and imagination.

- Decide what goals you have for yourself on this journey. Here are some examples:
  - I'm journeying toward a deeper relationship with myself.
  - I'm journeying toward a kinder internal narrative.
- Now determine how you are going to get there. For example, you might be aiming to:
  - Unlearn old patterns and create new ones.
  - Interact with my thoughts in a new way.
  - Consider my behaviors in a new way.
  - Process my emotions in a new way.
  - Experience success in a new way.
  - Approach challenges in a new way.
  - Interact with others in a new way.
- Ask yourself what it is going to feel like while traveling on this journey with yourself. For example:

- What do my thoughts sound like?
  - Am I self-deprecating?
  - Do my thoughts sound compassionate?
- What do my behaviors look like?
  - Am I being self-destructive?
  - Do my actions reflect how much I care about myself?
- How am I allowing my emotions to flow?
  - Am I ignoring my emotions? Am I exploring them?
  - Am I scared of my emotions?
  - Am I experiencing my emotions long enough to understand why the emotion is there?
- Reflect on how you will handle your successes along this journey. Ask yourself:
  - Am I celebrating my successes? If so, how? If not, why not?
  - Do I feel guilty when I succeed at something? If so, why?
- Now think about how you will approach challenges when they arise. Ask yourself:
  - Am I using my challenges as proof that I'm a piece of crap and will never amount to anything?
  - Am I understanding that challenges can be considered opportunities for growth and expansion of my self-awareness?
- Determine how you will care for yourself while working on your healing. Check in with yourself to ensure you are allowing time for rest and restoration. Ask yourself:
  - How do I feel about rest?
  - Does rest make me feel lazy? Who told me that caring about myself was lazy?
  - Is it uncomfortable to be kind to myself? Why?

These questions and examples can give you some guidance as you set out on your healing journey. Don't feel limited by these prompts, however—create whatever vision feels authentic to you!

## BEWARE FALSE, EXTERNAL VISIONS

A warning here: Many folks creating New Year's resolutions or vision boards create their goals around other people's perspectives. These visions typically have to do with weight loss, money, and cultural constructs (things like getting engaged or married, having children, buying a house, or going on vacations). Because of that, their visions are then based on the external, not the internal. Health, money, and families are amazing visions to have—*if* they are self-generated and manifested through your true authentic connection to yourself. But if they are generated from other people's perspectives, expectations, or assumptions about you, they do not truly represent your authentic, internal vision. When creating a vision, centering the OASIS concepts of authenticity and self-sovereignty can help stabilize this work. You are anchoring into your authentic needs and speaking your vision from a place of your own authority.

---

### Case Study: One Goal, Two Outcomes

Jack creates a vision board to help him build a better relationship with himself this year. One of his goals is to build muscle. He tells his friends that it's not because he wants to look attractive—it's because he knows he will feel better if he tones up a bit. Both things *can* be true, but let's see how it plays out. The italicized words following are explaining in a deeper way what is going on.

Jack is now a week into his workouts. He is hungry because he isn't nourishing his body well enough anymore (*he is rejecting his body's needs*). He has shooting pain in his shoulders. His legs are sore yet he continues to work out for two hours each day (*he is ignoring the signs his body is giving him to take it a bit slower*). He wakes up in pain on day seven—and he is angry (*anger is a sign that something is off internally with the goal and/ or the execution, yet most people project that anger outward and that is exactly what Jack does*).

Jack realizes he is pissed that he has to do these stupid workouts for other people to like him (*a sign that his original goal of "build a better relationship with himself" was actually a cover for wanting to get toned for a partner and not for himself*). He tells his buddy that he thinks it's absurd that women expect men to be toned and muscular all the time (*an all-or-nothing thought that is based on a generalization*). He says he is angry that men don't get dates if they aren't a specific body type (*a thought informed by a cultural construct of men's bodies and expectations from the external*). He is angry that he will never be good enough for women (*a belief turned inward because he is struggling with self-confidence, and instead of processing why he is struggling with self-confidence, the projection remains outward*). He starts resenting the workouts and resenting women (*a missed opportunity for self-growth, and an affirmation that the external will continue to craft the vision he has of himself*).

Here are a few examples of how the OASIS model can be used to untangle this example:

- Lacking self-ownership: Jack did not want to own the task of working out, and when things got hard, instead of claiming that he did not want to continue, he blamed women.
- Lacking authenticity: Jack was not authentic with himself about the reason he set this goal in the first place.

Jack's friend Henry also creates a vision board and puts building muscle on it as well. When he responded to the prompt about what makes him feel most alive, he wrote swimming. When Henry swims he feels powerful, he feels connected to his body, and he feels mindful. He realizes that he isn't able to swim as long as he would like to because his muscles have atrophied over the years, and he'd like to build up that strength and endurance again so he can do something he loves (*he is putting forth energy into his vision from an internal source*).

Here are a few examples of how the OASIS model can be used to untangle this part of the example:

- Exhibiting self-ownership: Henry acknowledged that he wants to swim to feel stronger and that the process will take some time because his muscles have atrophied. He is practicing radical self-honesty here as well.
- Exhibiting authenticity: Henry connected to the motivators that would help him remain committed to his goal when things get hard, and that motivator was based on building his strength, not based on other people's perceptions.

You can see the differences between how these two similar goals were conceived and executed. Self-generated goals are motivated by what's going on within you—they are not influenced or informed by your external environment (for example, other people's perspectives, opinions, judgments, or cultural constructs). Henry has set his vision from a place within himself, not from a place of someone else's expectation of him, and thus he finds more success.

## HOW TO SILENCE OTHER PEOPLE'S GOALS FOR YOU

It sounds easy to build goals that align with your internal and authentic self, but in reality, other influences can easily creep in. Why would someone else's goals for you be a problem? Setting your vision based on someone else's wants, needs, desires, or goals for you is taking away your authority, and because self-sovereignty and self-advocacy are vital to your healing process, it's important to build these emotional skills. People tell us what to do and who to be all the time. This sounds like:

- "You should focus on losing weight, then you'll be happier."
- "You should date my cousin; they are nothing like your ex!"
- "You should quit your job and move away; that will make you feel better."

The key here is not to try to block other people's advice but instead to tap into your perceptions and your needs. For example: If someone suggests that you should quit your job, remind yourself of your sovereignty and reflect on if that is a genuine option for you from your own autonomy, not because some random person told you to quit.

Everyone has advice—yet, no one is you. You are the only one who can tap into your deep, visceral needs. External sources often have mistaken views of your relationship because they don't have all the information—and thus they can't really know what's best for you. How many people thought you and your toxic partner were "as happy as can be"? They looked at your life without having the full context. They didn't see all the passive-aggressive fights, the manipulation, the slamming of doors. So when they say, "Why would you break up? You two were so happy!," you can practice your self-sovereignty and say, "I can understand how our relationship might have been easy to misunderstand because public perception was really important to my ex, but breaking up was truly the right decision." Be sure you do not allow other people's false and incomplete perceptions of you or your relationship to enter into your mind and sway your vision and goals.

## Exercise: Treat Yourself Like Your Best Friend Treats You

When you are creating your vision for the relationship you are cultivating with yourself, it can help to have prompts that set up what you're looking for. The following questions can be stepping stones to behaviors, traits, and patterns you want to embody.

- Envision someone you want to hang out with—such as a trusted friend or loved one.
  - How do they speak to you?
  - What kind of feelings do you experience after you spend time with them?
  - What kind of energy do they bring to the world and their relationships?
- Envision a true friend who you feel safe sharing your authentic truth with. Imagine you're having a conversation with them.
  - What does it feel like to be listened to?
  - What does it feel like to explore parts of who you are with-

out condemnation?
- What does it feel like to be radically honest about how you feel about certain things, people, and emotions?
- Identify parts of yourself that are currently being hidden.
  - Why are you hiding or covering up how you truly feel about something?
  - What would it look like to stop hiding these things?
  - Who do you feel safe to unmask around?

Review your answers to these questions. Although the questions invite you to think about other people, your responses will also reflect the type of relationship that you need to build with yourself. For example, if you said, "I need a friend that I can trust," layer in the examination, "Can I trust myself right now?" The answers will lead you to what areas you need to work on when cultivating a new internal voice.

## UNLEARNING YOUR DEFAULT REACTIONS

Your brain wants to automatically do certain things when it encounters specific situations—these are its default reactions. I also call them "linked mechanisms" because they show how your brain is closely connected to your habits. If it's not taught a new way to react, your brain will automatically default to these old reactions. These defaults can be thoughts, emotional responses, behaviors, or perceptions/assumptions that are informed by your past experiences, trauma, relationships, or things that were modeled for you.

Building a new vision for how your brain is going to interact with itself will mean that you need to unlearn old beliefs. You want to avoid inserting old, potentially toxic narratives into new situations. Identifying reactions that you can unlearn and unlink involves sitting with your immediate thoughts long enough to decipher and truly understand them. By practicing sitting patiently with your feelings, you can try to stop your automatic reactions and instead decide thoughtfully what to do next.

# Exercise: Identify Your Default Reactions

Before you can unlearn reactions, you'll need to identify which automatic reactions you currently have. This exercise will place you in imaginary scenarios so you can activate your default reactions. Read the questions and choose the answers that best fit your realistic reaction. You can pick more than one answer!

**Question 1:** When someone doesn't text you back immediately, what are your thoughts?
a. They don't care about this conversation.
b. They don't care about me (or value me enough).
c. They aren't by their phone.
d. They are by their phone but they aren't physically or emotionally available to respond to my text right now and that's okay.

**Question 2:** When someone backs out of plans at the last minute, what are your thoughts?
a. They don't want to hang out with me.
b. They found someone else better than me to hang out with.
c. They struggle with social events, so they may have been overwhelmed and backed out because of that.
d. I trust my friend and they don't have to justify changing their plans to me. If they aren't available, I am allowed to be disappointed—and at the same time, I know if they had been able to be here, they would have been.

Now take a moment and look at your answers. What might they tell you about the relationship you have with yourself right now?

For Question 1, let's pretend you answered option B—They don't care about me (or value me enough). Sit with that belief for a moment and explore your reaction. Ask yourself: Why did my mind say that one of my closest friends isn't answering my text because they don't care about me? Do I *really* believe that, or is that my mind speaking from a place of fear of abandonment? Could that thought be a default reaction from past relational traumas or past beliefs that are being applied to this current situation?

## Case Study: What Default Reactions Look Like

Mandy recently got out of a relationship that was very emotionally abusive and neglectful. Mandy is struggling with finding her footing again after the breakup because she realizes that her mind jumps to a lot of conclusions about people. For example, when she set up a date with Eric, a guy from one of her dating apps, he messaged her thirty minutes before the date and said he was running a little late. Immediately, Mandy was convinced he was going to stand her up. She spent the next forty-five minutes getting more and more angry at this guy that she had never met because she was convinced that he was not going to be fifteen minutes late as he'd said, that in fact, he was really just not going to show up at all. When Eric did show up, she was relieved, but she was still upset with him and she couldn't figure out why.

Default reactions are the thoughts that filled Mandy's head when Eric said he was going to be fifteen minutes late. Mandy felt scared she was going to be rejected. She got upset because she assumed Eric wasn't being honest with her. She got pissed that she put all this effort into doing her hair and makeup only to be stood up. These beliefs and thoughts are linked to past harm. Past relational trauma imprints itself on the mind. The mind will use its dominant pattern to react to current issues. So, because Mandy's ex-boyfriend constantly lied to her and didn't show up to events she had prepared for, Mandy is applying that pattern to her current situation.

Unlinking and unlearning default reactions is difficult because your mind is going up against very strong evidence that people can be cruel, manipulative, and deceitful—your past toxic relationship proved that. Unlearning default reactions sounds like saying to yourself: "Eric is late. There are many reasons why he could be late. He said he would be fifteen minutes late and I won't engage in any more assumptions or create any new expectations surrounding this situation until then."

## YOUR VISION IS NOT STATIC

The vision you have for the self you are working toward is meant to be reevaluated regularly. The vision you are creating today may change next month and that does not mean you have made bad decisions! Reevaluating your vision work is a necessary step to develop self-trust, emotional navigation, and self-discernment skills. Checking in regularly on your vision means that you are continuously tapping into your needs, which can change. Self-evolution isn't a linear journey—your path might have twists and turns but that's all part of the growth.

## KEY TAKEAWAYS

- Vision work must be specific, not vague.
- The vision you create for yourself provides a structure for healing the bond you have with yourself.
- What your internal voice sounds like must be considered when developing aspirations and goals for your self work. Think about the way you think about yourself.
- Default reactions (or linked mechanisms) are elements from the past that are being applied to your current situation.
- Unlearning default reactions is critical in healing the relationship you have with yourself and ultimately in developing healthy relationships with others.
- Reevaluating your goals and vision work is part of the healing process. You are allowed to reassess and realign your goals as they change.

## CHAPTER 9

# LISTEN TO YOUR VOICE

Your inner voice is always with you. Your inner voice refers to how your internal experience sounds to you—what you hear as your internal narrative. How does your voice speak to you? Many toxic relationships lead to inner self-talk that is judgmental, harsh, and discouraging. As you work to heal and rebuild your life, you'll need to reexamine this voice and learn to reframe it in a more positive light.

Like so many other results of toxic relationships, you must determine what's wrong before you can fix it. If you don't question how you talk to yourself, those narratives remain unexamined. Sitting with your internal voice while healing from harmful dynamics can make the difference between repeated attempts to heal and actually healing. At the end of the day, the way you interact with yourself can perpetuate either new or old cycles.

What is difficult after a toxic relationship is distinguishing your voice from their voice. Without you even recognizing it, your internal narrative can start to sound incredibly hurtful, mean, and ruthless—in other words, like your toxic partner. This is why we are spending an entire chapter on your voice. The shift you can initiate within your internal voice might be the exact pivot you need to jump-start your emotional processing and healing.

# WHAT'S YOUR HISTORY OF SELF-TALK?

Think for a moment. What does it sound like inside your mind? What does your inner voice say when it's reacting to stress, frustration, disappointment, or failure? Does the voice sound critical or cruel? Many people say, "That's just how I've talked to myself my whole life," but think hard…is that true? When you were a young child and you fell down, did you say to yourself, "Get up, you dummy!"? Or did you say, "I fell! This hurts, and I need help!"? At some point, your voice changed from neutrally experiencing situations to treating them with self-condemnation, self-deprecation, and self-criticism.

As kids, the external easily turns into the internal; so even if you grew up with very kind parents, if any influential human consistently exposed you to a critical narrative, your mind could have slowly shifted that voice that was at one time coming from outside to coming from within. Influences like coaches, grandparents, teachers, pastors, friends, or early romantic interests can contribute to this change. This chapter will tackle how you can change your internal narrative after you've spent years (possibly decades) engaging in unhelpful self-talk. We'll start by identifying whose voice is whose when you hear self-talk.

## Exercise: Determine Whose Voice Is Whose

Identifying what your internal voice sounds like and *who* it sounds like can be a huge pivot point in your recovery. Use the following exercise to help differentiate your voice from the voices of others. Answer the following questions with as many details as possible:

- How did your parents talk to you?
- How do/did other influential people in your life talk to you?
- How did your past partners talk to you?
- How do you talk to yourself now?
- How did your ex react when you were suffering?
- How do you talk to yourself when you struggle now?
- How did your ex react when you made a mistake?

- How do you process mistakes, perceived failings, and perceived setbacks now?
- Now imagine you drop a glass and break it:
  - What is your reaction? Do you believe it was just a mistake, or that you are stupid and clumsy?
  - If you think it was a mistake, does your inner dialogue say you are stupid anyway?
  - Does your inner voice allude to the idea that you shouldn't ever make mistakes, but if you do, you should be internally criticized for those mistakes?
- How does your inner voice sound when you make what you feel are bigger missteps?
- Does your inner voice speak with an all-or-nothing framework? This sounds like: "I'll never recover from this," "I always make bad decisions," or "This is why I can't trust myself."

Take a moment and review your responses. Your answers can help you understand who has influenced your self-talk and how it currently sounds.

## AVOID NEGATIVE SELF-TALK

As you begin healing, you also want to think about the way you are thinking about yourself. That may sound confusing, but it simply means that you should watch for any internal dialogue that's not supporting your goal or vision. When thinking about self-growth, many people hear a bully in their head. The voice is filled with angst and may sound nasty or discouraging. This is what a cold, unkind internal voice sounds like:

- "Shut up and get over it!"
- "You are a lazy slob—get up and go to your appointment."
- "You need to practice this stuff because you suck and you'll never get better if you don't practice."

How do those statements make you feel? Do you immediately feel resistance? Tension? Pressure? That very well might be your body speaking up against self-criticism and self-deprecation. Now let's do a short experiment. You're going to read those statements again, but this time, imagine your ex saying them:

- "Shut up and get over it!"
- "You are a lazy slob—get up and go to your appointment."
- "You need to practice this stuff because you suck and you'll never get better if you don't practice."

How do you feel about those statements now, hearing them through the voice of your ex? Do you get pissed off? Do you feel awful? Do you want to get to your appointment faster? Do you want to practice?

If this material resonates with you, know that negative feedback is yet another construct you were taught somewhere along the line—and that you can learn a different way. This may have even been the way your parents motivated you when you were a child. If they motivated you through voicing your deficits ("You're dumb; you need to study harder"), your mind has no other choice than to speak from this mindset rooted in negativity.

## CHANGING YOUR INNER VOICE FROM CRUEL TO COMPASSIONATE

Encouraging your inner voice to be kind and considerate will make every step of your healing journey a little bit easier. You want to speak to yourself in a way that allows space for trial and error. Anyone trying to grow and change will experience missteps and moments of difficulty and tension. If your mind sees that stumbling will be part of the journey toward healing, you will find yourself better able to overcome those challenges. You'll encourage yourself to keep going rather than put yourself down.

You are a human, and that means you will sometimes have to learn through hardship. No one is expected to show up to every difficult situation perfectly—and since you just came from a toxic situation, you may be especially sensitive to moments of tension. As you heal, you'll notice that your inner voice becomes stronger and better able to counter critical self-talk with love and compassion.

How can you reframe this critical voice? You can do that by acknowledging the challenge but reminding yourself that you can still make progress. For example:

- "Shut up and get over it!" turns into: "I hear you; this is painful. We must move forward, and you are right, moving forward will be hard."
- "You are a lazy slob—get up and go to your appointment" turns into: "You are struggling right now…we have an appointment in forty-five minutes and part of taking care of ourselves is getting to this appointment, and it feels difficult. That said, you deserve to maintain your health and you are important to take care of."
- "You need to practice this stuff because you suck and you'll never get better if you don't practice" turns into: "You are getting stronger and more aware every day. By practicing these skills, you are showing up for us and you should be proud of the hard work you are putting in to improve yourself."

Notice how an internal voice might use a variety of pronouns, such as *you, us, we, yourself,* and *ourselves.* That is okay! Depending on the situation and your phase of healing, different options might feel right at different times. This is self-advocacy in action. You are advocating for yourself instead of ignoring your needs.

## Using a Kind Inner Voice Doesn't Mean You're Lax

Speaking kindly to yourself is not the same as making excuses. If you feel a fear of making excuses for yourself, that is a narrative lingering from a past toxic dynamic. The compassion you feel from kind self-talk is validating the pain, honoring that the pain hurts, acknowledging how that situation is difficult, and trying new methods. As you do those things, you are learning and growing. An excuse, on the other hand, would elicit no new information or growth.

# THE PROBLEM WITH THOUGHT STOPPING

There was an old psychological process called "thought stopping" that was used for years in the psychology world. It describes the process of trying to tell yourself to stop thinking about something and was popularized by psychiatrist Joseph Wolpe in the 1950s. It was used to counter unhelpful or troubling thoughts, in hopes of interfering with the thought process. Thought stopping is considered by many in the psychology world as problematic because it unlinks a natural process that is attempting to occur. The brain is trying to process emotions, information, and experiences, and telling the brain to simply stop thinking about something can actually create more problems, namely "thought rebounding." Thought rebounding, a topic researched by social psychologist Daniel M. Wegner, is when a thought that was not properly processed comes roaring back into the psyche with a vengeance. The thought you attempted to suppress gains energy and force because your mind is attempting to keep it at bay. To counter thought rebounding, you must notice when you are thought stopping and you must allow the thought to be processed.

# DON'T INTERRUPT YOURSELF

In addition to thought suppression, interrupting yourself is another harmful narrative you may have been taught that affects your inner voice. It's a way of stopping your emotional processing and instead applying a harsh lens to the situation. If you attempt to process a thought, but your trauma or past wounds get in the way, you're likely to automatically respond with your negative inner voice. It's hard to notice because it's second nature to many people, especially those who have been in toxic relationships. Here are telltale signs that you are interrupting your own processing:

- **Invalidation:** Making the issue you are trying to process seem less relevant or frivolous to consider. For example, you might say to yourself:

- "That doesn't matter."
- "It's stupid to think about this."
- "This is so dumb, just stop caring so much!"

- **Devaluation:** Decreasing the importance of the issue you are trying to process, as well as decreasing your values around the issue. This sounds like self-talk such as:

  - "You shouldn't even care about this."
  - "You need to lower your expectations."
  - "It's not that big a deal."

- **Redirection:** Changing the focus of your processing as a way to disengage your original thought. Redirection self-talk sounds like:

  - "Aren't there more important things to think about?"
  - "Think about what they do right, not what they do that bothers you."
  - "Think positively!"

But thinking positively is a good thing, right? Well, as with everything, there is nuance. Yes, you need to consider the good things in a relationship as well as consider the harmful. But it's harmful to never consider your pain. Never considering your pain is interrupting your own processing and not allowing yourself to consider why you are struggling with a situation. In order to proceed with your healing, you'll want to work on making sure you don't interrupt your thoughts.

## HOW TO STOP INTERRUPTING YOUR THOUGHTS

Invalidating, devaluing, and redirecting are all tactics your mind uses to bypass emotional processing. Unfortunately, bypassing the difficult issues and tense moments won't resolve them or help you heal. Instead of automatically bypassing, take a moment to pause and ask yourself these "why" questions to help get to the root cause of your thought interruption:

- Why do I believe my thoughts don't matter?
- Why do I think I am stupid to consider my feelings about something?
- Why am I criticizing myself for caring deeply about an issue?

These questions will challenge your deeply held beliefs about yourself and consider the voice you are embodying when you are processing.

After you answer questions like that, you can start working to reframe your mindset and allow yourself to process challenging emotions. People who have endured relational trauma may have a fear response when they face painful emotions or difficult experiences. That trauma response may be because of past patterns that occurred when you attempted to process tense moments with your partner. For example, let's say you and your partner had a fight and you asked to talk about what happened. If your partner quickly snapped at you and said, "Ugh, you are so needy!," you may have shut down and gone quiet to keep the peace. Over time, if this happens again and again, that process trains your brain to switch off and give up on the task of processing the moment of tension because it caused you too much emotional pain.

In order to reactivate your ability to process difficult emotions, you must create safety inside of yourself. If you are upset with a friend, in the beginning of this process your internal voice might say, "Get over it! Why are you so sensitive?!" As you start to create internal safety, your voice will acknowledge that you are struggling, validate that struggle, and say something more like, "You are safe to feel upset right now. It's okay to process how you are feeling about what happened with that friend." That voice shifting into safety will open the door for more emotional processing.

*In order to reactivate your ability to process difficult emotions, you must create safety inside of yourself.*

## TRY THE CAVE METHOD

Another way to make sure that you fully process your thoughts is to apply the CAVE formula to what you just saw or heard. CAVE is an acronym I came up with to help you quickly remember the type of processing that is happening in the current moment. *CAVE* stands for:

- **C**onsider the conclusion you came to.
- **A**cknowledge what happened.
- **V**alidate the difficulty.
- **E**ntertain a different perspective.

Let's say you just got back from a date and your date spent the whole time criticizing various things about you, ignoring anything you said, and redirecting the conversation back to themselves. Afterward, imagine that your inner voice says, "Maybe they just had an off night. I'm sure they aren't this bad all the time." That *could* be true, but let's see if that statement holds up to some curious processing by applying the CAVE formula:

- **Consider the conclusion you came to:** This is where you'll review what happened and see if your initial conclusion is logical based on the facts. In this case, your inner voice might now say, "It sounds like you are doubting what you know you heard."
- **Acknowledge what happened:** Be radically honest with yourself. You might now say to yourself, "You didn't enjoy that date. They openly mocked you."
- **Validate the difficulty:** Recognize that disappointment and challenges are part of life. You might say, "You are allowed to be disappointed that the date wasn't a good fit."
- **Entertain a different perspective:** Use what you've observed, and process to see if there are any other possible conclusions besides "maybe they just had an off night." You might now say, "That probably wasn't one-time behavior; it was present all night. You don't deserve to be treated like that by anyone, especially someone who could turn into a partner."

Using the CAVE formula gives you a helpful framework to start challenging narratives that your inner voice might be sharing based on its experience in a toxic relationship. Plus, CAVE also strengthens your self-sovereignty.

---

## Case Study: Inner Voice Work

Jace (who uses they/them pronouns) has been broken up from their partner for a few months now. They had a partner who was hypercritical and very passive-aggressive. Their partner never wanted to communicate about issues and expected Jace to just simply predict their mood and act accordingly. Jace is now dealing with a lot of fallout from this relationship. For example, they are struggling to feel safe and secure lately, even around friends. Jace is constantly trying to read between the lines of friends' texts. Jace was attempting to have a gathering at their new place and here is how their text exchange with a friend named Ben went:

**Ben:** Hey Jace, sorry I can't come, I need a break. (*Jace immediately reads that as: I need a break from you.*)
**Jace:** Wow, that hurts. (*Ben is now confused.*)
**Ben:** Wait, what are you talking about?
**Jace:** If you don't want to be my friend then just say that.
**Ben:** Jace, that wasn't what I was referring to. I meant I need a break from socialization because I just got back from a family reunion. Of course I don't need a break from you.
**Jace:** Oh, okay. Sorry, I jumped to conclusions.

This is the point where Jace's internal voice is so important. Following are two ways this exchange could play out: one in which Jace uses a cruel and critical inner voice and the other with a curious and compassionate inner voice.

### JACE'S CRUEL AND CRITICAL VOICE
Notice how this voice is harsh, making assumptions, and doesn't believe Ben, even though Ben has never been dishonest with them in the past:

*Wow, way to make Ben think you are super dramatic. You could have just asked them to clarify what they meant instead of jumping to conclusions like an idiot. Now Ben is never going to want to hang out with you again because you overthink everything. Seriously, why would anyone want to hang out with you? You are annoying and paranoid. To be honest, Ben might have even lied to you about the family reunion because you are such an anxious, miserable person.*

### JACE'S CURIOUS AND COMPASSIONATE VOICE

This voice is validating, acknowledging emotions, gathering new information, and planning for ways to heal and grow from this misunderstanding:

*Jace, I'm curious...what happened with that interaction? Did you get scared they weren't coming because you thought they don't want to hang out with you? Does Ben care about you as a friend? In thinking about our memories with Ben, we know that they are super genuine and authentic. Ben hasn't ever lied to us, so that panic you felt when they wrote, "I need a break" activated something inside of us. That activation was from a very real and valid past experience with our ex. Remember how our ex never clarified? Remember how you always felt confused? That reaction to "I need a break" makes sense and we need to make sure we can navigate around that confusion. Ben cares about us. We have been friends for years. Ben might benefit from understanding that this reaction came from a place of trauma. With that in mind here are some options for us moving forward:*

- *We can talk to Ben about how some of the reactions we have are linked to past traumas and not current situations.*
- *We can talk to ourselves briefly when we feel activated and ask ourselves before we reply to a text.*
- *We can validate that our reaction is real and that our job is to not misappropriate the origin of that reaction to someone who is a stable, safe person in our life.*

> • *We can honor that sometimes these reactions will happen despite our healing. That's okay. In order to heal, processing (like we are doing right now) is the only way to gain the information needed to heal from activations like this.*
>
> Notice that with curiosity and compassion, the internal voice radically shifts into a healthy, safe processor and not a cruel persecutor.

## YOUR VOICE WILL GROW LOUDER AND STRONGER AS YOU HEAL

Your voice is one of the many parts of you that experienced trauma from your past relationship. Relearning how to listen to yourself, training your voice to be kind and compassionate, and processing difficult situations as they happen are key parts of reclaiming your voice. You're on a long journey of recovery, but all of your effort is worth it. Owning your inner voice can radically shift the trajectory of your life. You will be able to truly listen to your thoughts and treat yourself with kindness (which is not something you may have experienced in your toxic relationship).

That voice that comforts you and encourages you will now be with you all the time. You'll notice it become more confident, more knowledgeable, and more loving as you heal.

## KEY TAKEAWAYS

- Consider whose voice you are hearing inside your head when you are struggling.
- Being mindful of how past pain can show up in the processing of current situations or relationships can help you heal.
- The CAVE method is a quick resource when you are struggling in the moment with understanding how you are processing a situation.
- Nurturing a compassionate, authentic self-voice is key in allowing emotional processing, validating your experience, and establishing sovereignty over your healing.

# CHAPTER 10

# STRENGTHEN YOUR CONVICTION

*Believe in yourself! You can do anything! You can move mountains!!* Have you heard these phrases before? They sure sound great, but real life hardly ever feels like that when you're trying to heal from a toxic relationship.

The thing missing from all of these motivational statements is the *how.* Your inner voice is probably asking things like: "How do I believe in myself after years of being told I'm worthless?" Or, "How can I just accomplish great feats when I was told for years that I will amount to nothing?" and "How can I move mountains when some days I can't even move off the couch?" Let's be real. If healing from a toxic relationship was as simple as just saying "believe in yourself," this book would be a short one page! Believing in yourself and having conviction behind that belief takes time to develop.

This chapter follows the inner voice chapter for a reason. Strengthening your inner voice is what will power your conviction. So, what is your conviction? Your conviction is your *applied* belief. Conviction is not just you believing that you are worthy; it's you embodying that belief and applying that belief to your life. It's not just your belief that you can heal, but your fulfillment of that belief by showing up in a tangible way for yourself. Conviction is what shows up in your lived reality. Beliefs, without conviction, will stay in the mind. It is conviction that begs you to move forward and take back your power. This chapter explores how to step into the power of your own convictions.

# CONVICTION STARTS WITH BELIEFS

In order to get to conviction, you need to separate yourself from a few self-beliefs that aren't true. What do you believe to be true about yourself right now? If your beliefs about yourself are skewed, conviction will never come.

Let's look at some core beliefs that are common in people who are recovering from a toxic relationship:

- No one will ever love me.
- I have to shape myself around them in order for them to love me.
- I have to be easygoing and unbothered, or they won't stay.
- I am not good enough.
- I am too broken.
- I don't think people can really love the real me.

These beliefs aren't true. *No matter what happened in your past, you are worthy of love just as you are right now.* This truth may feel uncomfortable and implausible to you now as a result of your trauma, but in time, and as you progress with your healing, you will be able to believe that statement more and more.

## Exercise: Name Your Current Beliefs about Love

Ask yourself this question: "Do I believe that someone can genuinely love me?"

Write down your answer. It will speak volumes about the relationship you have with yourself right now and the way people have treated you in the past. Let's walk through three different ways people could answer this question.

- **Someone just beginning their healing process might sound like:** *No, I don't think I am good enough for someone to love me. I don't think I am attractive enough, I don't think I am funny enough, I don't think I have a good enough per-*

sonality, and I don't think I am rich enough, fun enough, or interesting enough.
- **Someone who is growing but lacks trust in themselves might sound like:** *I honestly don't know. Sometimes I love myself and think I am someone who deserves love, and other times I don't feel good enough at all. One moment, I care about myself and tell myself I am capable of being loved and then the next minute, I think the world hates me.*
- **Someone who has developed a healthy relationship with themselves might sound like:** *Yes. I am getting to know myself fully for the first time. I am not perfect and I am finally beginning to be okay with that. I love learning about areas where I can grow and I love learning about those things in other people too. I can accept that I am growing and that I will face challenges. I don't see those challenges as proof that I am not lovable; I see them as proof that I am human. I am capable of growth and self-evolution and I am worthy of being loved through that journey.*

Three different answers to that question; three different relationships to self. You may find yourself moving among the first, second, and third statements during your journey. Your progress doesn't have to be perfectly linear and you might move back and forth. Be gentle with yourself as you learn and grow.

## OVERCOMING DOUBT TO STRENGTHEN NEW BELIEFS

Think of relational trauma as the opposite of the gift that keeps on giving—it is the curse that keeps on cursing. Breaking a curse takes intention, skills, and effort. Breaking the toxic relationship curse looks like digging deep and reevaluating beliefs about yourself. These beliefs may have been so easy to believe when your partner was spewing them out left and right, but now you must work hard to understand that they're not true. This work will help you build strong convictions that stand up to challenges and obstacles.

## WHY YOUR DOUBT IS SO STRONG RIGHT NOW

Relational trauma feeds what I call the doubt dragon. Situations like these within toxic relationships feed the doubt dragon:

- When you doubt that you are worthy.
- When a partner neglects or gaslights you.
- When you doubt you are ever going to find someone who cares about you.
- When your partner says something hurtful like, "I don't care about your stupid hobby."

For some, that dragon was fed for years, if not decades, which explains why countering these beliefs is so difficult at first. You can point to every interaction with your past partner and/or even further back to relationships with fake friends or parents who lacked emotional depth. Those relationships were unskilled, emotionally illiterate, and lacked authenticity. Healing this wound deep within yourself will involve challenging that evidence, countering that "proof," and providing new information to replace old lies.

## REINFORCING DOUBT WITH SELF-GASLIGHTING

Self-gaslighting is when you try to convince yourself something is true when your authentic self knows it is not. Self-gaslighting can sound like the following inside your own head:

- Things aren't really *that* bad.
- Do you really think you deserve better?
- Maybe you aren't remembering correctly.
- Maybe you deserve this.
- You are just being dramatic.

When you are engaging in self-gaslighting, your authentic voice is typically being directly countered. That looks like this:

**Gaslighting self:** I am fine.
**Authentic self:** No, we aren't fine.

**Gaslighting self:** They didn't mean to call me a whore.
**Authentic self:** That was not an accident. This is a pattern you are ignoring, because being honest about the pattern means you may have to distance yourself from this relationship and we would rather live in a lie than be alone.

Self-gaslighting keeps a candle burning that was meant to be extinguished long ago. When you gaslight yourself, you are doubting yourself. You are trying to convince yourself that everything is okay and nothing needs to be processed or deeply considered. Self-gaslighting encourages you to turn away from your authenticity and truth. The more you self-gaslight, the more your life starts to feel fake, and the more you will feel internally conflicted. The pressure will build because your authenticity never goes away completely. It's the tension between your authenticity and the doubts fostered by self-gaslighting that creates that pressure!

## HOW TO ADDRESS YOUR DOUBTS

The way to address a critical wound like self-doubt is to go right to the source. Look for where your self-criticism is coming from. Does it have an external source or an internal source, or both? Notice if external influences are being given more power over your self-perception.

In order to fully stand in your beliefs and conviction, you need to have authority over yourself. If you are giving external sources authority over your authentic expression of self, style, voice, or opinions, you are forfeiting that authority. Acknowledging yourself as an authority over your life can feel scary at first, especially when coming out of a toxic relationship. But establishing self-agency is exactly what leads to conviction of your truth.

## Case Study: Two Approaches for Dealing with External Influences

Blair is a few months out of a very emotionally toxic relationship. She is struggling with the belief that she is not pretty enough to find another boyfriend. She is focused outward, looking for validation of her beauty from others. She has very low self-worth and doesn't see her own opinion as valid. She goes on a few dates and hears some feedback: One date said she was too short, another said they prefer blondes, and the last one said he didn't like her style. Blair got angry and impulsively bought high heels, got blond highlights, and bought a few new outfits. She repeats this cycle depending on whatever feedback a date gives her. Blair is looking at herself as a problem to fix, and she is seeking the solution to that "problem" from external sources. Blair lacks self-authority and self-sovereignty.

Clare is also a few months out of a very emotionally toxic relationship. She is struggling to find someone who connects with her unique sense of style. She loves a lot of florals and bright colors. A few guys send her DMs telling her she looks like a grandma, and another one said he would be embarrassed to be seen in public with her. Instead of looking at herself as something to change for a guy, she realizes if she changes for them, they are dating her for what they can turn her into, not for someone she actually is, in this moment, as her authentic self. Clare applied the strategy of curiosity and ultimately prioritized her authentic passions and desires. Clare is exhibiting self-sovereignty and authority over her self-expression.

Blair and Clare have two different beliefs about themselves. Blair believes she has to adjust herself to match what other people want. Clare is able to allow herself to be who she is and wait for someone who can appreciate that. When you are early in the process of your healing, you might feel connected to Blair's approach. But as you learn and grow, you might find yourself feeling more confident and able to try Clare's approach.

# HOW SELF-TRUST CAN BUILD CONVICTION

So far in this chapter, we've talked about how to determine where your beliefs about yourself are coming from and how to reclaim control of your beliefs. The next step will be applying these beliefs in real life—in other words, your conviction. As you bridge the gap between believing in yourself and having conviction, you'll find that you need to trust yourself. Applying your beliefs takes an incredible amount of trust that you are capable of making decisions for yourself. This trust takes time to develop and nurture. Your toxic relationship eroded your foundation of self-trust, so you will need to work to build it back up.

Let's say you want to go back to school. It takes a lot of courage to go back to school, because that means you have to trust yourself enough to commit to the coursework you are studying. What if you don't like it? What if you make it a year in and then decide that you don't want to study this topic anymore? What if the coursework gets too difficult? Those are all very valid questions, and those are all very real issues that come up when making big decisions like whether to go back to school!

As you emerge from a toxic relationship, it can feel uncomfortable and scary to take a chance like this on yourself. It's key to reassure yourself that you are not always going to have everything figured out, and that's okay. Trusting yourself to make a leap like going back to school is a big challenge—in many cases, it's easier to just maintain the status quo and keep doing what you're already doing. But if the status quo isn't you living an authentically happy life, that's not fair to you.

## Extract What You Can from Every Situation

Look at your life as something to observe with a curious mind, and envision yourself extracting useful knowledge from every scenario. Even challenging situations offer opportunities to learn important bits of information about yourself and your life that you can use as a basis for growth. Using this type of mindset will help you begin to trust yourself and your choices because you can always learn something from them.

Self-trust involves:

- Giving yourself space to try, and to not necessarily be successful at everything. Give yourself permission to start over.
- Not forcing yourself to go against everything inside of you. If you want to try something, try it.
- Being honest with yourself.
- Connecting to your true self and listening to your needs.
- Believing that you are strong enough to get through challenges.

When you acknowledge and meet your needs, you build self-trust. Even the process of healing from a toxic relationship can help you build self-trust—with that work you show yourself that you believe you're worth the effort and that you deserve a happy, fulfilling life. You know what's best for you because you did the work—you left a difficult situation, changed harmful narratives, and reconnected with your inner voice.

*The process of healing from a toxic relationship can help you build self-trust—with that work you show yourself that you believe you're worth the effort and that you deserve a happy, fulfilling life.*

## Case Study: One Choice, Two Different Perceptions

Will decides to move out of state. He has wanted to do that for years and is finally going to take the plunge. He got a job that is remote so he has the flexibility to move. After he settles in, though, things start to feel off. He realizes quickly that he didn't take into account how much he values being close to his family. He starts to get upset, thinking that he made a bad choice and shouldn't have signed a yearlong lease. He doubts his ability to make decisions because for years he'd thought he wanted to move, and now that he has moved, he immediately realized that he wants to move back as soon as he gets the chance. He feels ashamed of himself and thinks he is foolish, makes bad decisions, and was stupid for taking this chance.

Manuel decides to move out of state. He has wanted to do that for years and is finally going to take the plunge. He also has a remote job that offers him flexibility to move, so he does. After he settles in, he starts to miss his family. He realizes that there was no way he could have understood just how much he values being close to family without actually being separated from them. He looks at his choice through the lens of curiosity and learning. This experience of moving taught him that he highly values his family. Before this move, he wasn't sure how much he needed to be close to his family. He listens to himself and starts to make plans to move back home once it is possible.

It is your perceptions that fuel doubt and distrust within the self. Consider that Will and Manuel undertook the exact same action, but they walked away with two very different conclusions. This is not a mistake—your past informs your perceptions. One person saw a failure, which leads to self-doubt, and the other saw a learning opportunity, which builds self-trust.

## THE OTHER SIDE OF CONVICTION

When you start practicing applying the beliefs that you have reframed about yourself, things are going to start to happen. On the other side of conviction are people who will challenge you. The people who will challenge your newfound convictions never walked in your shoes, they never endured the relationship you just were a part of, and they never knew your partner or saw the things you saw. When an external source challenges your conviction, it's not going to feel good. It's honestly going to feel horrible. You have probably even experienced a variation of this. Here's an example:

> **Your conviction:** I am so glad I am no longer with them.

> **The challengers:** What are you talking about? Your ex was the nicest person I've ever met! They always made me laugh when we all hung out together! Honestly, you lost a catch!

This might be coming from a coworker, a friend, your mom, or a sibling, but regardless of who challenges your conviction, this is where the real work comes in. You *will* have people doubting your narrative. They won't believe your truth. They will misunderstand your motives. They will even try to insert a new narrative over you, saying things like, "Your loss. It's hard to find people that make you laugh!" This is probably the most important part of embodying and applying your newly founded beliefs: Allow them to misunderstand you. Remain constantly anchored in your own story. Never take your narrative out of context.

## YOUR CONVICTION IS SO POWERFUL

The conviction you are now working to achieve was hard-fought. Every single tear you shed, every single sleepless night, every single painful conversation was giving you the information that allows you to say with conviction, "I will not be treated like that ever again." This is self-advocacy in action.

The more you believe that and apply that belief to your actions, the stronger your healing will be. Conviction is an especially powerful part of the process because it bolsters and deepens your healing. Feeling this confident won't happen overnight but it is worth your effort and focus in order to hold your head high, trust in your choices, and live authentically.

## KEY TAKEAWAYS

- Your convictions are your beliefs applied to everyday life.
- If you constantly doubt yourself, the relationship you have with yourself gets weaker.
- You can counter self-gaslighting by listening to the way you speak to yourself and by taking an inventory of the kinds of beliefs you hold about yourself.
- Self-trust is built over time by listening to yourself, showing up for yourself, and taking your needs seriously.
- Part of learning how to navigate your own decisions is allowing yourself to learn from a choice that wasn't right for you without weaponizing that decision as proof that you make bad decisions.
- The stronger your convictions, the less likely external misunderstandings about your convictions will hold weight. You know what's best for you. Let your conviction be your power.

# CHAPTER 11

# ESTABLISH YOUR NEW STANDARD

You are working hard to recover from the harm you've experienced, and now it's time to explore what a healthy relationship should look and feel like. You have thus far spent a lot of time focusing on establishing what a healthy and safe relationship with yourself looks like. Now let's discuss what a healthy and safe relationship feels like with another person.

You will use many of the same tenets that you used to build your vision in Chapter 8 to imagine a future partnership. Just as you resolved to treat yourself with love, kindness, and respect, you will also look for that from a new partner. This chapter will walk you through many categories of preferences, such as communication, socializing, sex, and managing conflicts. You'll decide what you are looking for in a new partner—and practice your new skills of owning your power, listening to your needs, and trusting your decisions.

## EMOTIONAL CONSENT

You have probably heard about the concept of consent as it relates to interacting with people sexually; emotional consent is a less commonly discussed concept but still very important. Emotional consent involves asking another person if they have the capacity to hold a difficult conversation or emotional dialogue, and it is important to have this for any relationship to thrive. You can practice emotional consent in any relationship, but friendships, family relationships, and partnerships are the most common places you'll be using it.

In practice, emotional consent looks like texting your friend, "Hey, I just had a really hard conversation with my mom, are you in a place to hear a heavy story tonight?" This gives the friend time to reflect on what their capacity is at the moment and if it's possible for them to enter into a lengthy dialogue.

### What Needs Consent

To be clear, emotional consent is useful to ask for with heavy dialogues, not every dialogue. Use your discretion—you would most likely not need to ask for emotional consent when dialoguing with your partner about where to order takeout, but you may want to ask for emotional consent when dialoguing about whether or not to start couples therapy.

Practice emotional consent right off the bat if you can, in newer friendships and in newer partnerships. This could even happen on a first date. The date asks, "Tell me about your family." This seems like a prompt that could go anywhere, so ask a clarifying question and then follow with emotional consent. This looks like: "My family is a heavy topic...are you able to chat about a heavy topic right now?" To some, this may seem intense, but the alternatives don't provide much emotional value. Let's look at what some possible alternative responses might be:

- Say nothing of value; skim over the question ("Oh, my family is fine").
- Dive into deep, intense reflections about your family (this might overwhelm them).
- Redirect the question to them, saying something like, "Oh, that's not important, you tell me about yours!"

All those alternatives would contribute zero value to the bond you both are trying to form with each other. Asking for clarification and consent can help the conversation flow in a direction that both parties have consented to.

If you are asking your partner for their emotional consent to discuss a difficult topic, they could say, "No, I'm not able to have that conversation." Here is the nuance: If you are in a relationship with someone who is consistently refusing to hold space for difficult conversations, they are communicating something by omission. What that "something" is may vary, but if they are consistently saying no when you ask them if they are able to have a hard conversation, they are telling you that they don't have the emotional capacity to connect with you in the depth that you are requiring.

This is where your standards come in. You are allowed to have a relationship that has emotional depth. You are allowed to seek a relationship with someone who can hold space for difficult conversations. So if you find yourself in a situation where you are asking for emotional consent and consistently being shut down, after attempting to hold space for why that pattern is occurring, it is perfectly reasonable to tell your partner that this is an important skill that you value in a partner and because of that changes need to happen.

## Case Study: Emotional Consent in Everyday Life

Ray gets home from work and immediately starts unloading a very heavy conversation onto Riley. Riley didn't even get a chance to say hi to Ray before he launched into his issue at work. Riley asks Ray if they could take a breath and circle back to this conversation after dinner. Ray felt rejected when Riley asked to have the conversation at another time. Ray is starting to practice curiosity around tension he feels, so when he starts asking, "Why am I experiencing tension right now?," he realizes a few things:

- He never asked for Riley's emotional consent.
- He immediately expected Riley to be in a place to have a heavy conversation.
- He didn't acknowledge Riley in any way when he got home.
- He felt defensive when Riley calmly asked him to have to conversation after dinner.

Ray is showing signs of self-ownership in this reflection. Emotional consent can be a lifesaver for relationships that are recovering from past toxic relationships because it allows autonomy to enter the conversation. Ray realizing he got defensive and never gave Riley a chance to consent to the heavy dialogue they just got thrown into is a game-changer. Because Ray is working on balancing Riley's needs with his needs (meaning, Ray is working on interdependency), he is recognizing that asking for emotional consent is essential in order to create a healthy dialogue around heavy issues.

## HOW TO ESTABLISH RELATIONAL STANDARDS

Now that you are in the process of listening to your inner voice, trusting yourself, and living your life with personal conviction, you are in a good place to establish the standards you want a partner to meet in future relationships. These are called relational standards. In order to start establishing a firm sense of how you want someone to interact with you in an intimate relationship, you need to break down, in very specific detail, every part of the relationship. As licensed clinical social worker and couples therapist Patricia Lamas said, "A relationship is made up: It doesn't exist on its own. It's imagined and cocreated. We have to make sure we are imagining and creating the same relationship." The following exercise will help you and your new partner explore your relational standards together.

## Exercise: Record Your Relational Standards

This will be an extensive exercise but it's really important to consider all of these topics. Take your time and go through these questions at your own pace. They don't need to be answered in one sitting.

Also, as you progress in your healing, these answers may change, and that is okay. Your healing is an evolution. You can and should continue to update these answers throughout your healing journey.

Ideally, you'll answer all of these questions on your own, your new partner will do the same, and then you can review your answers together to start the conversation around relational standards and expectations moving forward. *You are not always going to agree on every point—that doesn't mean you're not a good match.* The process of discussing these details is helpful in and of itself. Even if you're not in a relationship now, it's still valuable to do this exercise on your own.

### ENERGY STANDARDS

- Do I get my energy from others or from being alone?
- Am I an introvert, extrovert, or ambivert (a combo of the two)?
- If I could choose between an introvert, extrovert, or ambivert, which one would I want my partner to be?
- How do I feel when my partner is low on energy?

- Can I respect that sometimes my partner's energy levels will not match mine?
- Am I able to dialogue with my partner about energetic discrepancies between the two of us?

## SOCIALIZATION STANDARDS

- How much socialization do I need?
- How much socialization do I hope my partner needs?
- How much socialization can my partner engage in with other people?
- What are some hobbies I'd like us both to have that may involve socialization?
- Do I expect my partner to join my hobby/special interest/culture?
- Am I able to discuss what we'll do when a socialization discrepancy occurs (for example, my partner wants to go out but I don't)?
- How do I want my partner to respect my autonomy surrounding my free time?
- Do I expect my partner to do everything with me?
- Do I want my partner to expect me to do everything with them?
- If I am not interested in something my partner wants to do socially, how do I want them to react?

## EMOTIONAL PROCESSING STANDARDS

- How do I typically process emotions?
- If my processing style does not match my partner's, how will I assess the way my partner processes?
- Am I able to discuss my wants and needs around processing conflict, tense moments, or difficult conversations?
- Is my partner able to hold space for emotions without guilting, shaming, or judging me?
- Am I able to hold space for emotions without guilting, shaming, or judging my partner?
- Do I show skills around emotion identification and emotional processing?

- Does my partner show skills around emotion identification and emotional processing?
- Do I give my partner space and time to process conflict or tension?
- Does my partner give me space and time to process conflict or tension?
- Does my partner demand answers during a conflict?
- Do I demand answers during a conflict?
- Do I think certain emotions are "bad" emotions?
- Do any of my emotional processing strategies help me process emotions and also harm me (for example, self-harm)?
- Do I see my emotions as something to endure or something to process?
- What kind of parameters am I placing around my emotional processing (for example, *I am not allowed to cry*; *I don't get to be angry*).

### Different Kinds of Emotional Processing

People can process emotions in different ways—verbally (talks through it with you), in a written way (sends you a bunch of text messages/writes a letter/email), or internally (becomes more quiet and it takes time for them to come to a conclusion). The differences between an external processor and an internal processor can come into play in a relationship as well:

- People who prefer **external or verbal processing** usually talk through their emotions. They also tend to reflect faster, almost in the moment, but their initial thoughts or emotions after a conflict may change to something different a few hours later.
- People who prefer **internal or reflective processing** usually think about their emotions internally. They may also take more time—they may not fully process during the actual conflict.

## SEXUAL STANDARDS

- What are my sexual needs?
- How do I view sexuality?
- What are my views on porn?
- What are my thoughts on self-pleasure/masturbation?
- How do I feel about my partner engaging in self-pleasure/masturbation?
- What are my expectations if a pregnancy occurs in our relationship?
- Do I experience any discomfort around sex?
- Have I discussed any past traumas involving sex and how they can be navigated during sexual intimacy with my partner?
- Do I have shame discussing my sexual needs?
- How much sex would I want?
- How would I discuss differences in sexual expectations with my partner?
- How do I define intimacy?
- What are things that I see as intimate that aren't sex?
- Do I like to:
  - Cuddle?
  - Hold hands?
  - Be flirted with?
- Have my partner and I discussed the parameters on interacting with people of the gender we are attracted to?
- What do I consider flirting?
- What do I consider emotional infidelity? Be as detailed as possible here! Is my partner:
  - Able to be friends on social media with the gender they are attracted to?
  - Able to be in-person friends with the gender they are attracted to?
  - Able to "like" pictures on social media of the gender they are attracted to?
  - Able to text or message with someone who is the gender

they are attracted to?
- If all my answers are no, have I explored fears around infidelity and issues with trusting a partner?

## COMMUNICATION STANDARDS

- What does communication in a healthy relationship look like to me?
- Would I like the communication between my partner and me to happen primarily in person?
- Do I consider texting an acceptable communication method in a relationship?
- What does it look like to establish a mutual baseline of healthy communication?
- Do my partner and I perceive communication in different ways? Be specific here. For example: Does my partner see communication as a simple "How is your day?" and I see communication as something deeper, like discussing emotional needs?
- How do I define "consistent communication"?
- How frequently would I like to communicate with my partner?
- How are we mutually agreeing on our communication needs?

## PLAYFUL/BONDING STANDARDS

- How important is humor and playfulness to me in a relationship?
- What are some concrete examples of how I would like to create space for levity, humor, and playfulness in my relationship?
- How will I dialogue about any playfulness discrepancies that might occur (for example, my partner wants to tickle me and I'm not in the mood at the moment)?
- How would my partner have fun if they weren't with me?
- How would I have fun if I weren't with them?
- What activities could we do together that encourage playfulness and joy?

- How will I feel if my partner participates in a hobby or an activity that they enjoy but I don't?
- How might we dialogue about different perceptions around free time?
- Do I feel guilty when I am relaxing? If yes, why might that be?

## STANDARDS FOR CONFLICTS

- How do we agree to talk to each other during a conflict?
- Have we discussed emotional consent?
- Is yelling acceptable?
- Is mockery acceptable?
- Is it acceptable for us to use harsh language or swear during a conflict?
- Is slamming doors and throwing items acceptable?
- Are we establishing limits on how long a difficult topic will be discussed?
- How can I check in with my energy and stress levels during a conflict?
- What cues might my body be giving me as indicators to pause and revisit the conflict at another time?

## LET YOUR STANDARDS BUILD A SOLID FOUNDATION

Standards for a potential partner are not mere hopes and wishes that you eventually want. Standards are anchored points of established expectations. By creating and discussing these anchor points, you can gain more psychological stability in your relationships.

You should revisit your standards when you are in the early stages of a relationship—when you're more likely to feel flustered and excited. Standards ground you when that type of longing could cause you to ignore red flags along the way.

Then, if the relationship grows more serious, you can ask your partner to complete the survey and discuss the points together. As you talk, you can get a better idea of how your partner and you can coexist in a relationship. The beautiful thing is that you are designing this relationship together. By creating open dialogues like this and creating safe places to process difficult issues that may arise, you are also able to incorporate new standards and expectations as they come to light. Those changes won't be viewed as a threat because you both have normed the expectation of coming together and discussing any shifts that are occurring.

## WHEN TO COMPROMISE

When you are developing your standards, you will be interacting with the dynamic of self-trust. In terms of relational standards, love is not meant to be unconditional. That is a recipe for abuse. Relationships must have boundaries *and* those boundaries are meant to be established after you have developed a deep understanding of your own needs. After you have a good sense of your needs, you can use that information to help determine what is something you are authentically willing to compromise on and what is a deal-breaker.

A compromise in a healthy relationship does not ask a partner to deny a core authentic part of themselves. A partner can appear to ask for a compromise, when in actuality they are requesting you to become the person they imagine you to be in their head. For example, your partner can ask you to go camping with them, but if you have told them that you've been camping before and really don't enjoy it, they're essentially just asking you to suck it up and fake it. This is why compromises aren't to be taken lightly.

Compromise on things that don't disrupt your authentic truth. So if you have a partner who tells you, "Well, I wanted a partner who camps with me," you can tell them, "I'm not willing to fake my enthusiasm to soothe you," and that might be the deal-breaker because you confirm you aren't what they are looking for. This is a scenario in which compromise would not have been appropriate; so many people compromise when they really need to be clarifying who they are and what makes them tick. If they do not clearly understand that, partners will compromise, compromise, compromise into a person they don't even recognize.

> ### Looking at How Far You've Come
>
> After you finish the Record Your Relational Standards exercise in this chapter, it might be interesting to review your answers to the Identify Your Relationship Norms activity in Chapter 1. You will likely see how much your mindset has changed as you processed your emotions and healed.

## ARE YOUR STANDARDS TOO HIGH? (ANSWER: NO)

As you begin dating again, you might hear a common phrase from friends or loved ones: "Your standards are too high." Consider what that really means to you and if you truly want to take it to heart. If you lower your standards, you will ultimately be seeking people who are not what you authentically want. When you start off a relationship in an inauthentic way, you are setting up both parties to be resentful of each other. One person is angry that their new partner is not rapidly evolving into who they envisioned them to be, and the other person in the relationship is pissed that their new partner is attempting to change them all the time.

### WHAT IT LOOKS LIKE TO LOWER YOUR STANDARDS

For the sake of that argument, let's play along and imagine lowering your standards. Let's pick a random question from the exercise on relational standards you just completed and discuss what it looks like when you lower that standard: *Is it acceptable for us to use harsh language or swear during a conflict?*

If your preferred standard is that it is *not* healthy to add this kind of language into a conflict with your partner, but you allow it with your next partner thanks to lowering your standards, that means you could be exposing yourself to what amounts to verbal abuse. Lowering your standards may seem like it's not a big deal, but it can have massive psychological implications.

So, while society may laugh and say, "You're never going to find someone who meets all your standards," you can just ignore this negative external influence and then emotionally process any self-doubt. Remind yourself that the only way to maintain a sense of safety and stability in your future relationships is by establishing standards and sticking to them. Fall back on your conviction and belief in yourself and hold your head high.

> *Remind yourself that the only way to maintain a sense of safety and stability in your future relationships is by establishing standards and sticking to them.*

## WHEN YOUR NEW PARTNER MAKES A MISTAKE

We are all human, so mistakes are going to happen. Let's say you and your new partner decided to not swear at each other during a fight and that plan seems to be working well. Then, a few months into your relationship, your partner slips and calls you a name during a fight.

First, it's important to be able to dialogue about what occurred and process any issues that arose. In an ideal world, your partner would hold themselves accountable, acknowledge that they crossed a line, and apologize sincerely. Many times, though, people aren't able to do that right away. What typically happens is that you get upset—both because you got called a name by someone who claims they love you, and because your partner failed to acknowledge their mistake. So, because you aren't willing to lower your standards anymore, you bring it up. If your partner is able to acknowledge that they crossed a line, that is a very good sign. If your partner gets upset that you are attempting to maintain the standards both of you set together, it's important to examine whether that mindset fits with your relational standards. Highlight that you are not trying to condemn your partner for a mistake, but attempting to maintain the standards that you both established together.

## WHEN YOU MAKE A MISTAKE

Again—no one is perfect. Despite all your hard work and healing, you may be the one who slips up. If you, say, cussed out your partner during a fight, take a moment to emotionally process the event. Several thoughts might arise:

- Are you scared that you are being held to that standard, but they aren't going to honor it on their end? If that is true, discuss it.
- Are you scared that they will leave you if you screw up again and that by discussing it, you are drawing more attention to it? If that is true, why is that fear there?
- Are you angry when someone points out opportunities for self-growth and accountability? Where is that anger coming from?

If you did make a mistake, apologize for it. You are still worthy of love, and you are still growing and learning. Remember, challenges are part of the process.

If, on the other hand, you are struggling to maintain the standards that both of you set, give that topic some thought. Don't automatically assume you are the bad guy. Standards change sometimes. Is there room for you to discuss these changes in your relationship? The problem that occurs in a lot of relationships is one person changes the standards and doesn't update the other partner on what is going on. Maintaining and changing standards takes communication, and lots of it!

## CREATE, DEFINE, AND ALLOW FOR GROWTH

Standards aren't meant to feel like rigid rules that take all the fun out of a relationship. They are meant to help shape and define the partnership you two are cocreating. Once you've identified your standards, take them seriously and give them top priority.

Nontoxic relationships should be safe spaces that allow for conversing through tension points. You should both feel comfortable acknowledging issues and also helping each other to see meaningful opportunities for growth. Both individuals need to embody self-ownership over their actions. Both individuals must want to foster interdependency in the relationship and not codependency. Both individuals must acknowledge how their past trauma may show up in the relationship. This type of relationship is possible—and you deserve it!

## KEY TAKEAWAYS

- In order to develop relational standards, you must have a firm sense of how you want to be treating yourself, and then move on to how you want others to treat you.
- Use the Record Your Relational Standards exercise to deepen your understanding of the standards you want to establish.
- Engaging in new standards with a new partner is a learning process. It takes time, communication, and lots of self-awareness to establish and maintain relationship standards—but it's worth the effort!
- Mistakes happen. How you and your partner address and/or take ownership for those mistakes will help indicate the emotional health of the relationship.
- Standards can and will change. Healthy relationships work to establish a safe working space to discuss any changes in the standards.

# CHAPTER 12

# EMBRACE YOUR NEW NORMAL

The relationship that you have been building with yourself throughout Part 2 of this book is one that places high value on your well-being, pleasure, pain, and experience; your perspective and your peace are paramount. In other words, you are the most important factor to consider when you think about love. Even as you look for—and hopefully find—a loving partner, you need to love yourself. That deep bond with yourself is what will anchor you into your standards and into your new conceptualization of relational norms.

i already fell in love with myself
i'm ready to be with somebody
who can do the same
fall in love with me
*how i did*

—Kia Marlene, @kiamarlene

## WHAT A NEW NORMAL LOOKS LIKE

It's now time for you to experience healing relationships that once seemed out of reach. A new normal looks like:

- No longer speaking to yourself in a cruel way.
- Holding your standards high.

- Saying, "I am powerful enough to ensure this self is treated with the dignity it deserves."
- Being curious, compassionate, and courageous.

It takes immense courage to keep walking forward; know that on the other side of this work are people who have walked a similar road and are hoping to find someone like you who has done this work as well.

---

### Recalibrating Your Threshold

Creating a new normal is coming to the realization that sometimes your trauma and pain threshold is too high. Things that you have considered "normal" in a relationship may never have been healthy. In order to heal, your brain and body must start to become more attuned to when they are being injured. This is difficult because it's easy to see a physical injury, but it's very difficult to register an emotional injury. The goal here is recalibration. Recalibrating means deciding what you are no longer going to tolerate and then activating a boundary to enforce that new threshold.

---

## FINDING SAFE PEOPLE

Finding a safe community of people who exhibit safe ways of interacting is a very important part of your healing journey. The term *found family* is gaining traction in the psychological community for a reason—because for many people, their own family has never been able to provide them with psychological safety. Found family members are typically made up of friends who you know can provide a safe environment for you while you are on your healing journey, and beyond.

What are some things to look out for when you are cultivating your found family and forming a psychologically safe community? First, let's look at some signs that tell you that someone may *not* be able to give you psychological safety:

**Red Flags**

- You feel like you have to mask your authentic self when you are around them.
- They mock you or your emotions when you are being expressive.
- They talk about people behind their back, particularly about what they wear, what they look like, or who they hang out with.
- They use "always" or "never" phrasing (for example, "I never do that" or "I always do that").
- They one-up you in conversations (for example, you say you didn't sleep well and they say, "Well, I only got three hours of sleep last night, stop complaining").
- There is a lot of confusion in your friend group (for example, people are constantly saying they "heard different things from different people" and things aren't adding up, which is a sign of lying, deception, or omission of truth).

On the other hand, here are some signs that someone *is* able to provide psychological safety:

**Green Flags**

- You feel mentally relaxed around them and safe to be authentically you.
- They are able to see multiple truths co-occurring at the same time (for example, you can be depressed and wake up and go to work every day).
- They are kind and compassionate around people's pain and people's experiences.
- They don't jump to conclusions if you are late, if you are slow to text back, or if you forget to reply to something.
- They ask for clarification about issues instead of assuming (for example, they ask if you accidentally forgot to tag them in that social media picture—instead of assuming that you purposefully excluded them to hurt them).
- They trust you.

- They talk through their emotions with you and you feel safe to do the same with them.
- They genuinely celebrate your successes and get excited when good things happen to you.
- If any conflict occurs, they are able to dialogue through any issues without deprecating you or treating you poorly.

If your friends are also in trauma recovery and they have normalized harmful behaviors, they may not see emotional red flags either. Establishing a healthy community is part of the healing process because you don't want to work so hard to heal and then immerse yourself back into a community that criticizes you for changing or showing up in a new way. Your community should support you, not cause you more pain.

*Establishing a healthy community is part of the healing process because you don't want to work so hard to heal and then immerse yourself back into a community that criticizes you for changing or showing up in a new way.*

If you are finding yourself showing up as a person you don't want to be in your friend group, that is a good sign that you may need to shift who you associate with. As you heal, you are going to notice more behavioral patterns because your awareness has expanded. Things you didn't previously think were problematic will now look like big problems. That is the point—but also a painful part—of awareness. This does not mean you have to walk away from all your friends or dump your current partner—but it does mean that you need to be mindful about who you choose to spend your time with. Protect your physical and emotional health above all else.

## Case Study: Awareness Leads to Tension

Caden has been married to his partner for ten years. Caden has been doing a lot of work on himself as well as attempting to be more mindful in his relationships with others, including Julie. Caden has always known that Julie loves to be sarcastic and jokes around all the time, but it wasn't until recently that Caden realized just how much Julie would use jokes as a way to put him down in front of his friends and family. Previously, Caden just thought Julie had a weird sense of humor and he would just let the jokes slide off his shoulder. Now that he is tuning inward to how those jokes impact him, he is noticing that every time Julie starts talking at a family event, he freezes up. When he started to get curious why he was so tense around his wife at social events, he realized that it was because he was afraid she would randomly make underhanded jokes about his clothes, his hair, and his job at the dinner table. Caden realizes now how much tension he experiences due to these constant "jokes."

Caden is showing signs that he is not normalizing the jokes anymore. His new normal gave him a new sense of awareness surrounding the implications of the jokes that his wife says. Caden decides to tell his wife what is going on: "Julie, I want you to know that those little jokes you make about my 'goofy hair' and my 'boring job' really affect me. I didn't realize it until I started asking myself why I was so tense at family gatherings."

Julie has a choice here. If Julie chooses a defensive and unhealthy way of receiving this information, she might respond like this: "Well, you need to get some thicker skin, 'cause life is tough." With those words, Julie essentially said, *I don't have any problem continuing to be your bully and you are going to have to continue to endure this pain because I don't see any issue with it at all.*

If Julie chooses a healthy way of receiving the information about how her jokes hurt Caden, it might sound something like this: "I never realized how bad it was getting. You don't deserve a bully for a wife. I am going to be more mindful of how I show up. I'm grateful that you brought this up to me because I don't want to be the reason you are struggling mentally."

# WHEN NEW STANDARDS LEAD TO TENSION

The reason why conviction is the last stage of healing is because when someone realizes that their pain is valid, they have to go beyond simply being aware and use their conviction in order to initiate real change. The only way your new normal is going to be sustained is through activation of new skills and new strategies in your life, and those skills start with awareness and self-advocacy.

## PAY ATTENTION TO TENSION

Your new normal is based on paying attention to situations that make you tense, and also to those that don't. You are now noticing when:

- Something makes you feel unsafe or uneasy.
- You are being spoken over.
- You feel authentically like yourself.
- Someone is able to process *with* you, not against you.

When tensions arise, you now know that is a sign to see what's going on emotionally and process it using your curious mind. Could you be struggling with self-advocacy or self-sovereignty? What emotions are behind that event? What was the context in which your tension occurred? Always give yourself consent to continue asking questions and processing until you feel you understand what happened and why.

# PRACTICE SELF-CONSENT

Just as you want to get consent from a partner about various things, you can also ask for your own consent as well. For example, if you start to get upset about something, you can ask yourself, *Am I able to hold space for processing that for a few minutes right now?*

By practicing self-consent, your mind can feel more of its own sovereignty and power. The fascinating part of self-consent work is that the more you ask yourself if you are ready to process, the more your mind will feel capable of navigating pain in small bits and pieces, instead of all at once. You are asking yourself to try to process traumas, painful emotions, and difficult situations for a few minutes at a time. Giving yourself a time frame of how long you will endure that pain can make the task feel more bearable and achievable.

## Exercise: Try This Five-Minute Tension Processing Activity

In this activity, you will find a tension point for yourself (this could be a recent conflict or difficult event) and ask yourself if you are feeling able to process that tension for five minutes. You can even set a timer. To process the tension, you might write down everything that came up for you surrounding that tension, allow yourself to cry about the pain, or breathe and ask yourself curious questions. Flow with the energy your body is presenting you with and make sure you are able to do this alignment work in a private area.

By asking yourself if you are able to process for a few minutes, and by saying yes and giving yourself a time frame for that processing, you allow your brain to start to feel stabilized around that processing. You are clarifying your consent to your brain around your processing of that trauma.

### ASSIGN YOUR TENSION

Instead of ignoring it, suppressing it, and/or pretending it's not there, assign a place for your tension to go. The tension was there for a reason and the information you get from it is important. Once you know what it is, find a place for it to be worked through. Ask yourself, *Where might I best process this tension?*

Here are a few ways to process tension points:

- In therapy.
- Asking for your friend's emotional consent and then talking through the issue with them.

- Through movement (dance/stretching/massage/light exercises).
- Via written processing (write down the tension, wait a day, then reread what you wrote).

Remember to go into these spaces with intention. For example, if you want to process some tension you have around your job in therapy, keep that intention at the forefront of your mind so you can actively target that tension and not get off topic and start processing something else five minutes into the session. Making a plan to deal with inevitable challenges is a healthy part of living post-trauma.

## KEY TAKEAWAYS

- When you are building a new normal, treat yourself as a high priority.
- Your self-exploration and self-development do not have to end when you enter into a partnership.
- Building a safe community of family and friends is a fundamental building block of toxic relationship recovery.
- Being mindful of relationship red flags helps you notice if a person may not be a psychologically safe person to bond with.
- Healing is painful because your awareness of problematic behavior expands.
- Giving yourself consent to process trauma in small ways and identifying ways to process tension are good ways to approach difficult processing without reliving similar trauma narratives from your past.
- Your recovery stems from deeply bonding and aligning with yourself.

# CONCLUSION

You have come an extraordinarily long way from your toxic relationship. Remember, you are doing this work to reclaim the pieces of yourself that relational trauma took. You are doing this work to remember what has been deep within you the whole time: your value, your potential, and your power.

Toxic relationship recovery is not about running away from a toxic dynamic and hoping you never come across another one. Toxic relationship recovery is about reclaiming yourself. It's identifying your authentic self and looking right at it and saying, "I will fight for you to exist again."

You are exactly where you need to be. You are the navigator and it's time to step into your power and take back what is rightfully yours.

# GLOSSARY

**ALL-OR-NOTHING MINDSET:**
A tendency to think only in extremes and with an "either/or" filter.

**ANXIOUS ATTACHMENT:**
People with an anxious attachment style will constantly seek reassurance about the relationship.

**APPEASING TEASING:**
When a person does not develop relational skills and stops at "awareness," essentially leading their partner on and being intentionally manipulative.

**BLAME-SHIFTING:**
A form of deflection that's used when a partner is asked to hold themselves accountable for an issue or a problem; involves shifting the conversation drastically into an offshoot of the original issue.

**BOTH/AND MINDSET:**
A mindset that allows you to feel two things at the same time.

**BUFFER:**
Anything, such as gifts, that deflects you and your partner from processing the real issues that are going on in the core of your relationship.

**CAVE:**
An acronym to help you quickly remember the type of processing that is happening in the current moment. It stands for: Consider the conclusion you came to; Acknowledge what happened; Validate the difficulty; Entertain a different perspective.

**CODEPENDENCE:**
Enabling and not allowing the other person to develop needed skills to be independent.

**COLLECTIVE HEALING:**
When groups of people understand the oppressive and exploitative systems that surround them and refuse to normalize harmful procedures, policies, and practices in that system.

**COMPLEX TRAUMA:**
Prolonged, repeated trauma that causes harmful disruptions in a person's identity formation and sense of self.

**COVERT TRAUMA:**
Trauma that is difficult to see at face value.

**DEFAULT REACTIONS:**
The automatic ways your brain tends to respond when it encounters specific situations.

**DEVALUATION:**
Decreasing the importance of the issue you are trying to process, as well as decreasing your values around the issue. This also can refer to devaluing you as a person and treating you poorly in the relationship. In addition, devaluation is part of the idealization/devaluation cycle in love-bombing.

**DRIP:**
An acronym to help you remember the particular nature of complex trauma; it stands for duration, repetitive, insidious, and persistent.

**EMOTIONAL CONSENT:**
Asking another person if they have the capacity to hold a difficult conversation or emotional dialogue.

**EMOTIONAL DISSONANCE:**
The disconnect between what you know deep down and what you have normalized.

**EMOTIONAL PIGGYBACKING:**
When your partner sees your progression and expects you to teach them all you know and then acts as though they are healing by proxy.

**EMOTIONAL PROCESSING:**
A method of reflection and introspection that helps you transform an emotional experience or feeling into useful information for your psyche to consider.

**ENMESHMENT:**
Blurred boundaries and entangled lives (everyone knows everything about everyone and no one is allowed privacy).

**EXTERNAL INFLUENCES:**
Goals, expectations, or beliefs created from other people's perspectives, expectations, or assumptions about you.

**EXTERNAL OR VERBAL PROCESSING:**
When a person processes emotions by talking through them.

**GASLIGHTING:**
When a person manipulates someone into questioning their own sanity.

**HARMFUL ACCOUNTABILITY:**
Needing to report to your partner where you are at all times—in other words, a lack of personal autonomy and relational trust.

**HARMFUL DISCLOSURE:**
The act of oversharing information with your partner, to the point of losing your sense of privacy in the relationship.

**HARMFUL RELIANCE:**
Relying on a partner for things that should have been nurtured within yourself.

**INDIVIDUAL HEALING:**
Healing that occurs in personal, inner worlds, addressing past perceptions, past beliefs, and past behaviors.

**INTERDEPENDENCE:**
Mutually integrating yourself with others without losing yourself.

**INTERNAL OR REFLECTIVE PROCESSING:**
When a person processes emotions by thinking about them internally.

**INVALIDATION:**
Making the issue you are trying to process seem less relevant or frivolous to consider.

**LOVE-BOMBING:**
The act of trying to exert power and control over another person's life through excessive displays of love early on in a relationship.

**NEGLECT:**
A relational method where one partner withholds engagement, love, time, effort, or their presence to get what they want.

**OASIS:**
A model that examines the development of healing after trauma through the layers of complex interactions that occur within the self. The acronym stands for ownership (of self), authenticity, self-sovereignty, interdependency, and self-advocacy.

**PARENTIFICATION:**
The act of treating a child like an adult throughout their childhood.

**PRIVACY:**
A healthy way to honor internal and external boundaries while allowing for individual development.

**RADICAL SELF-HONESTY:**
The practice of connecting with the authentic reason why you employed a certain defense mechanism or trauma-informed skill, disengaged from a situation, or engaged in any other potentially harmful behavior.

**REDIRECTION:**
Changing the focus of your emotional processing as a way to disengage your original thought. Redirection can be done internally or it can be used on you by a partner to avoid difficult conversations.

**RELATIONAL STANDARDS:**
Details that outline how you want someone to interact with you in an intimate relationship.

**RELATIONAL TRAUMA:**
Trauma that occurs within the interpersonal dynamic between two people. This is trauma *in* the connection.

**RELATIONAL WOUNDS:**
Faulty constructs that shape your conceptualizations of what a relationship should feel like or be like, what is deemed acceptable or tolerable, and what is normalized. Collectively, they are the components of relational trauma.

**SECRECY:**
Not disclosing information that is necessary for both parties in the relationship to be aware of.

**SELF-ADVOCACY:**
Speaking up for yourself.

**SELF-BLAME:**
Blaming yourself and taking full responsibility for a relationship breakdown.

**SELF-CONSENT:**

Asking for your own permission to enter a situation or conversation. Self-consent can also be applied to your own trauma processing. This involves asking yourself if you are ready to enter into difficult or painful emotional processing. When you ask for self-consent, you are honoring your autonomy.

**SELF-GASLIGHTING:**

When you try to convince yourself something is true when your authentic self knows it is not.

**SELF-OWNERSHIP:**

Taking control of your story and the relationship you have with your own trauma.

**SELF-SOVEREIGNTY:**

The authority you have over yourself.

**"STINGS":**

That feeling when someone tells you something that is meant to build you up or genuinely be nourishing to your psyche—but you immediately refute or downplay it.

**THEMATIC DEPTH:**

Finding a deeper understanding about yourself or certain issues.

**THOUGHT REBOUNDING:**

When a thought that was not properly processed comes roaring back into the psyche with a vengeance.

**THOUGHT STOPPING:**

The process of trying to tell yourself to stop thinking about something.

**TRANSACTIONAL LOVE:**

Love based on a give-and-take mindset.

# SOURCES

Bakker, G.M. (2009). "In Defence of Thought Stopping." *Clinical Psychologist*, 13(2). https://doi.org/10.1080/13284200902810452.

Brower, K. (2010, December). "The Danger of Cosmic Genius." *The Atlantic*. www.theatlantic.com/magazine/archive/2010/12/the-danger-of-cosmic-genius/308306.

Burns, D.D. (1980). *Feeling Good: The New Mood Therapy*. New York City: William Morrow and Company.

Herman, J.L. (1993). *Trauma and Recovery: The Aftermath of Violence—from Domestic Abuse to Political Terror*. New York City: Basic Books.

Minuchin, S. (1974). *Families and Family Therapy*. Cambridge, MA: Harvard University Press.

Overstreet, N.M., & D.M. Quinn. (2013). "The Intimate Partner Violence Stigmatization Model and Barriers to Help Seeking." *Basic and Applied Social Psychology*, 35(1). https://doi.org/10.1080/019735 33.2012.746599.

Strutzenberg, C.C., J.D. Wiersma-Mosley, K.N. Jozkowski, & J.N. Becnel. (2017). "Love-Bombing: A Narcissistic Approach to Relationship Formation." *Discovery: The Student Journal of Dale Bumpers College of Agricultural, Food and Life Sciences*, 18(1). Retrieved from https://scholarworks.uark.edu/discoverymag/vol18/iss1/14.

Wegner, D.M., D.J. Schneider, S.R. Carter, & T.L. White. (1987). "Paradoxical Effects of Thought Suppression." *Journal of Personality and Social Psychology*, 53(1). https://doi.org/10.1037/0022-3514.53.1.5.

# IMPORTANT RESOURCES

## NATIONAL INTIMATE PARTNER VIOLENCE RESOURCES

### UNITED STATES NATIONAL DOMESTIC VIOLENCE HOTLINE
The National Domestic Violence Hotline is a 24-hour confidential service for survivors, victims, and those affected by domestic violence, intimate partner violence, and relationship abuse.
Call: 1-800-799-SAFE (7233)
Text: "START" to 88788
Live Chat: www.thehotline.org/get-help/#

### NATIONAL DATING ABUSE HELPLINE
1-866-331-9474

### FINDING LOCAL RESOURCES
Enter your location details and check which services you are looking for in your area.
www.thehotline.org/get-help/domestic-violence-local-resources

### CREATING A SAFETY PLAN
Read carefully through the steps and be mindful when printing the plan or adding information on a computer with data history and search history. If possible, use a public computer that can't be traced back to you.
www.thehotline.org/plan-for-safety/create-a-safety-plan

# SPECIFIC COMMUNITIES RESOURCES

### THE INDIGENOUS COMMUNITY
StrongHearts Native Helpline
1-844-7NATIVE (1-844-762-8483)
https://strongheartshelpline.org

### THE BLACK COMMUNITY
Ujima: The National Center on Violence Against Women in the
Black Community
1-844-77-UJIMA (1-844-778-5462)
https://ujimacommunity.org/find-help

### THE LATINA/LATINO/LATINX COMMUNITY
Casa de Esperanza
Linea de Crisis (24-Hour Bilingual Crisis Line)
1-651-772-1611
https://esperanzaunited.org/en

### THE DEAF COMMUNITY
The Deaf Hotline (24-Hour ASL Crisis Line)
1-855-812-1001
www.thedeafhotline.org

## TEEN SUPPORT

### LOVE IS RESPECT HOTLINE
This US government service is provided by the National Dating
Abuse Helpline. The 24/7 hotline offers confidential support for
teens, young adults, and their loved ones seeking help, resources,
or information related to healthy relationships and dating abuse in
the United States.
Call: 1-866-331-9474
Text: "LOVEIS" to 22522
Live Chat: www.loveisrespect.org/get-relationship-help/#

### SAFE DATES MATTER

Safe Dates Matter is an education campaign for teens about dating violence, with the realization that one in three high school students experience physical and/or sexual violence by a significant other.

https://safedatesmatter.org

## COLLECTIVE RESOURCES FOR COMMUNITIES AND INSTITUTIONS

### THE CENTER FOR RELATIONSHIP ABUSE AWARENESS

The Center for Relationship Abuse Awareness educates communities, institutions, and young leaders to take collective action against gender violence.

https://stoprelationshipabuse.org

### LEGAL RESOURCES

A list of resources related to various legal issues such as divorce, child custody, and restraining orders.

https://stoprelationshipabuse.org/professionals/legal-professionals/legal-resources

## SUPPORTIVE APPS

### ASPIRE NEWS APP

This app is disguised for safety. It allows users to set up a way to call for emergency support. Users can prerecord a voice message or create a text message that can be automatically sent to designated entities if the user feels unsafe or that they are in danger. It also has a feature that allows the recording of video or sound if abuse is actively occurring.

www.whengeorgiasmiled.org/aspire-news-app

## SAFENIGHT APP

This app provides a way to support victims of domestic violence and the services and organizations that help them. Through the app you can donate directly to shelters or pay for a night's stay for someone fleeing a violent situation.
www.safenightapp.org

# MORE FROM THE AUTHOR

## UNLEARNED PODCAST

Dive deeper into trauma recovery with Jaime's podcast, available on Apple, Spotify, or anywhere you listen to podcasts.

# INDEX